For more than a generation now we have sought to attract and entertain our precious youth rather than nurture them by grace. The majority have responded by turning their backs on the church. Brian Cosby has listened to their heart and is offering us the best biblical guidance we could ever hope to receive.

—**Michael Card,** Award-winning Singer, Songwriter, and Author

For decades the church has allowed the tail to wag the dog in regard to youth ministry. We have attempted to find the answer to every problem facing teenagers by flooding money into bigger and flashier programs. The results of our efforts speak for themselves. I am thankful that Brian Cosby steps forward in *Giving Up Gimmicks* and does something that has been unheard of: marrying solid biblical theology to youth ministry methodology. If you are concerned on any level about seeing young people in your church build a faith that will last, then I highly recommend this book to you.

—**Danny Mitchell,** Youth and Family Ministries Consultant and Associate Pastor of Discipleship and Youth, New City Fellowship, Chattanooga, Tennessee

John Williamson Nevin once critiqued Charles Grandison Finney's revivalism by distinguishing Finney's "system of the [anxious] bench" with historical Protestantism's "system of the catechism." One philosophy of ministry looks for quick results while the other looks for gradual, sustained growth. One is based on ingenious methods while the other is based on God's methods. As a former youth pastor, I know that most models of American youth ministry are systems of the bench and are not saturated with the Word, sacraments, and prayer. Yet these are precisely the anchors that the souls of our youth need. These are precisely what Brian Cosby calls us back to. I thank God for this book.

—**Daniel R. Hyde,** Pastor, Oceanside United Reformed Church

The percentage of students walking away from the church after high school is staggering. This book not only identifies the "whys" but gives applicable, biblical ways for the church and youth leaders to address this challenge head-on. I would recommend this as a must read for anyone concerned about the next generation.

—**Jay Shaw,** Youth Pastor, Briarwood Presbyterian Church, Birmingham, Alabama

Structuring a modern youth ministry by following the contours of Scripture and keeping the body of Christ at the epicenter? What a novel idea! Yet this is just what Brian Cosby has done. And the result is radical and refreshing because the Bible remains cutting-edge in every culture. If you want true success in your ministry, here is the thought-through operational blueprint.

—**R. Kent Hughes,** Senior Pastor Emeritus, College Church, Wheaton, Illinois

If you are serious about making a lasting impact in the lives of your youth and preparing them for the long haul of life, *Giving up Gimmicks* is a must read. Brian Cosby understands how the ordinary means of grace change young people, draw them closer to Christ, and build a foundation that will last.

—**Rod Culbertson,** Associate Professor of Practical Theology, Reformed Theological Seminary, Charlotte, North Carolina

Brian Cosby believes that youth ministry should be based on the same means of grace that nurture the whole church.

This book contains good theology that reflects his conviction that strong biblical doctrine will grip and transform the lives of youth (and others). So don't read this volume just as a handbook on how to minister to others—*you* will find yourself challenged and strengthened by reading it! I commend him for writing it, and recommend it to youth workers and others for their personal growth as well as effective ministry.

> —**Joseph Martin,** Professor of Biblical Studies and Ministries, Belhaven University, Jackson, Mississippi

In *Giving Up Gimmicks*, Cosby boldly reminds the church of her God-given responsibility (and privilege) to minister to our youth on God's terms. The means of grace—Word, sacraments, and prayer—are the verdant pastures where our Good Shepherd, Jesus Christ, feeds and nourishes his flock . . . youth included! In these pages, therefore, Cosby provides us with something exceedingly rare, namely, a clear, cogent, and compelling articulation of biblical youth ministry! I warmly commend this book.

> —**Jon Payne,** Minister, Grace Presbyterian Church; Lecturer, RTS Atlanta

In our entertainment culture in which the church often looks like the world in order to draw the world into the church, Brian Cosby offers us a much-needed word about the identity, purpose, and strategy of effective, God-centered youth ministry. A pleasure to read, this book brims over with winsome anecdotes, gospel-driven applications, and passionate pleas to recover biblical understandings on Holy Scripture, sacraments, spiritual discipline, and Christlike community. For those who desire the gospel of Jesus Christ to permeate the lives of a new generation, this book is a must-read.

> —**Christian George,** International Speaker, Author

The "traditional" approach to youth ministry has treated youth like autonomous individuals unrelated to their families or the church. The youth of the church are first and foremost members of the church, "covenant children" as they've come to be called, because they are members of Christian families. Youth ministry, then, if properly done, is family-centered and church-centered. It trusts that God works through families and through the ordinary ministry of the church. Finally, we have in Brian Cosby's *Giving Up Gimmicks* an approach that does justice to the family and the church, while providing practical helps for youth workers.

—**Terry Johnson,** Senior Minister, Independent Presbyterian Church, Savannah, Georgia

GIVING UP
GIMMICKS

GIVING UP
GIMMICKS

RECLAIMING
YOUTH
MINISTRY
FROM AN
ENTERTAINMENT
CULTURE

BRIAN H. COSBY

P·O. BOX 817 • PHILLIPSBURG • NEW JERSEY 08865-0817

Library of Congress Cataloging-in-Publication Data

Cosby, Brian H.
  Giving up gimmicks : reclaiming youth ministry from an entertainment culture / Brian H. Cosby.
    p. cm.
  Includes bibliographical references and index.
  ISBN 978-1-59638-394-4 (pbk.)
  1. Church work with teenagers--Presbyterian Church. 2. Church entertainments. 3. Grace (Theology) I. Title.
  BV4447.C62 2012
  259'.23--dc23
                                    2011042960

To Doug, Tim, and Norm:

wise mentors, faithful friends,
and champions of the means of grace

CONTENTS

FOREWORD

ALMOST ALL OF US are aware of the encouraging and inspiring accounts of Daniel (Belteshazzar), Hananiah (Shadrach), Mishael (Meshach), and Azariah (Abednego) found in the book of Daniel. In 605 BC these four youths were suddenly and unceremoniously uprooted from their families, their country, and all familiar surroundings by a conquering pagan empire known in history as Babylon, ruled by the notorious King Nebuchadnezzar. They were then submitted to an assimilation process designed to culturally revolutionize their lives socially, religiously, and politically to make them royal servants of the king and his imperial designs. These four youths were assigned pagan names, enrolled in a pagan international school, and placed under an inflexible curriculum encompassing religion, philosophy, and every sphere of life, even one's diet, supervised by a royal official from the king's cabinet.

The first six chapters of Daniel reveal their courageous yet thoughtful and faithful commitment both to their God and to his glory. They were bold without arrogance, and they were humble without reticence. They became a significant lifestyle statement for the glory of God and an asset for the general welfare of the king and his empire, as well as a vibrant witness of the transforming power of God's grace before the watching world. Even more, they established an encouraging testimony to the exiled people of God in Babylon. Their influence and impact were demonstrated repeatedly by their courage to be faithful to the Lord their God in worship and witness, while simultaneously becoming an instrument of God's providence in the lives of believers and God's common grace in the lives of unbelievers. They stood the test of fidelity to God-centered worship by refusing to participate in a royal diet supplied by pagan-worship sacrifice. Furthermore, their unflinching trust in God's providence was visibly demonstrated by their refusal to worship the king's idolatrous image to the point of being cast into a "fiery furnace." Their faithfulness and God's deliverance not only penetrated a pagan empire but was ultimately used as a vital part of God's work of grace in the conversion of Nebuchadnezzar himself. These four youths became ambassadors of the King of kings to a hostile king in the context of a rampaging imperial kingdom. Furthermore, their witness continued through multiple dynasties and even another conquering empire, the Medo-Persians under King Cyrus.

Interestingly, all four of these youths were, at the time of their exile into bondage, the same age as the teenagers who populate our junior high youth groups. Would it not be appropriate for you and me to ask ourselves a searching question? What would the teenagers in our youth groups do if they also were uprooted by a pagan and/or atheistic conquering nation and sent into a sophisticated effort to transform their life view and lifestyle? Without wanting to become too controversial, I would like to ask another question: aren't our covenant children who are heading into today's institutions of learning also being challenged by a pagan, secular world and life view that denies the claims of Christianity—sometimes intellectually and many times with mockery—and seeks to transform the way they have been taught to think and live in their homes and churches? How do we prepare them for such adversity so they do not simply survive but thrive, and like Daniel, Shadrach, Meshach, and Abednego become salt and light in the midst of darkness?

I am convinced the answer to how our covenant youth will respond to the inevitable challenges of atheistic secularism and neo-paganism will normally be determined by what has already been invested in their lives. This gospel evangelism and disciple-making will enable them to face what the evil one intends to be a life catastrophe and transform it into a moment of growth in the grace and knowledge of Christ our Lord. The unassailable fact is that people do not become at the moment of adversity something different from what they are. At the moment of trial we do what have become the habits of our hearts. The habits of the hearts of our covenant youth are divinely designed to be nurtured in their families, their extended families, and their church families as the gospel of grace first calls them to Christ evangelistically and then equips them to live for the preeminence of Christ consistently in days of prosperity and/or adversity.

From the fullness of biblical truth revealed in the New Testament, it is abundantly clear that Daniel, Shadrach, Meshach, and Abednego were trophies of the gospel of grace, who became both instruments and witnesses to the power of that gospel of grace. The untold story hinted in the names they had been given by their parents was about the role of their families and of the precursor of the local church that was established by regional teaching centers (later giving birth to synagogues during the Babylonian captivity itself). The family and "church," working in concert, had prepared them for moments of trial, adversity, and decision. These extraordinary young men of God were the products of God's grace, which we can biblically assume had been applied with some consistency as they were raised in "the nurture and admonition of the Lord."

The gospel of grace produces extraordinary testimonies of grace by the regular and prayerful administration of the ordinary means of grace such as the preaching and teaching of God's Word, the fellowship of God's people, and the gathered worship of the covenant community, all bathed in the communion of the saints and the regular employment of intercessory prayer. The family, equipped by the church through the means of grace and the church extending the family's ministry with the means of grace, produces men and women of God who will live imperfectly yet intentionally to the praise of the glory of his grace.

You are about to begin a much-needed journey in the pages of this book. The journey will outline how we can reclaim the intentional ministry of the gospel of grace through the means of grace in the lives of families, all enhanced by a ministry to the youth of the covenant and then through them to the world by employing God's ordained means of grace, which the world calls foolishness but out of which God makes saved sinners "strong and courageous" as well as "humble and loving."

The coming generation is ready for us to bring them to Christ through the gospel by the means ordained from Christ, so they are enabled and empowered to live for the preeminence of Christ with courage and boldness that despise arrogance and with humility and compassion that embrace the strength of the Lord. Your journey begins now.

Harry L. Reeder III
Senior Pastor, Briarwood Presbyterian Church

PREFACE

THE GOAL OF THIS BOOK is to give youth pastors, youth leaders, and parents a guide on how to lead a gospel-rich youth ministry that incorporates the means of grace—Word, prayer, sacraments, service, and community—into the content of the ministry as well as its methodology. Much of the material in this book has been hammered out "on the field" over the last decade or so of working with youth in various ministry contexts. But this book is certainly not the product of one person. Many have helped shaped my approach to youth ministry, especially Norm Dunkin at Carriage Lane Presbyterian Church in Peachtree City, Georgia. In fact, it was he who first asked me to write this book.

Giving Up Gimmicks: Reclaiming Youth Ministry from an Entertainment Culture is not designed to be an exhaustive manual, but rather an approach to leading and nurturing teenagers by ushering them unto the green pastures of God's transformative grace. All too often, youth programs have turned to entertainment-driven models of ministry in order to bring in the most youth as possible to the local church. Success has become the name of the church-growth game. The devastating effects, however, are seen not only in the number of youth leaving the church after high school, but also in a spiritually and theologically shallow worldview among many American teenagers. The irony is that these same teens actually *want* to grow and learn hard truths. They want to know how to think about suffering, how to pray, and why Jesus had to die.

American youth also have a deep desire to be known and loved. They want truly intimate relationships that are committed, safe, and glorifying to God. They want to experience grace in community and grace in the gospel. Moralism won't cut it. Just being a nicer person hasn't saved anybody, and it surely won't cultivate a teen's relationship and communion with Christ. Teens need to know that they are far more sinful than they would ever imagine. But, through faith alone in Christ alone, they are far more accepted and loved than they would ever dream.

After explaining some of the trends in youth culture, I examine the theology and support for the means of grace and then take the reader through each of the "means"—providing both biblical understanding and practical advice on incorporating them into a model of youth ministry. I conclude the book with a chapter on how to impart this vision to others and how to build a ministry team that is committed to fostering the means of grace in their own lives as well as the lives of youth.

May God grant a modern Reformation of youth ministry across America that seeks faithfulness over success, the Word over entertainment, and God's glory over our own.

1

WHY ENTERTAINMENT HASN'T WORKED

"ARE YOU GOING TO spank your kids?" was the first question. As I stumbled for an adequate answer, "Of course!" fumbled out. I didn't have any children at the time, but the room was packed with young examiners probing areas I usually didn't talk about. But I wanted to make a good first impression.

I was being interviewed for a youth pastor position at Carriage Lane Presbyterian Church in Peachtree City, Georgia. I had already completed a phone interview and written questionnaire, and now I was visiting the church for a three-day *thorough* interview process with the search committee, the Session of elders, and now the students.

After a barrage of random (and I mean *random!*) questions came my way, one teenager finally raised his hand in the back of the room. "Are you going to hold us to high standards?" A little shocked and wanting him to clarify, I asked him to repeat his question. "Will you challenge us as our youth pastor?" he said with greater intention. I was both stunned and delighted.

In preparation for the series of interviews, I had been reading every book I could get my hands on relating to youth ministry, including the well-known *Purpose-Driven Youth Ministry* by Doug Fields, former youth pastor at Rick Warren's Saddleback Church in Lake Forest, California.[1] Although I had already been a youth pastor for several years before this interview, I felt like I needed to brush up on the "how-tos" of youth ministry.

I had scoured the pages of countless books on youth games, ice breakers, and strategies to attract the largest number of youth to a church. The key theme that I found in many of these books envisioned a youth program that centered on making youth group as *entertainment*-driven as possible with a message on Jesus "slipped in" somewhere.

After I arrived in Peachtree City, I happened to sit in on a meeting of various youth pastors planning a big ecumenical weekend event. The first hour was spent talking about which "Christian magician" to invite. The group spent the next ten minutes selecting a speaker, who invariably needed to be "funny." After hearing reports that all the youth who went to this event experienced a spiritual revival, I started questioning whether I should have supported it. But, it only took a week before those high-on-Jesus youth fell back into their same old patterns at school and indicated very little, if any, lasting effect.

THE GRADUATES' GREAT EXODUS

In his book, *Battle Cry for a Generation*, Ron Luce estimates that "88 percent of kids raised in Christian homes do not continue to follow the Lord after they graduate from high school."[2] The drive to elevate experience over truth within a youth-group worship time has caused youth pastors to spend through the roof on fog machines, circulating lights, and artistic backgrounds. In the end, the show has left the teenager with some teary eyes and perhaps a newfound commitment that he or she will never sin again. But the next morning it's all over, and they are left wanting something deeper, richer, and more satisfying.

The numbers are staggering for those leaving the church after high school, yet youth ministries across the nation continue to pack in more and more pizza parties and video games to keep youth coming back—thinking that somehow their lives will be changed.

Since that awkward and semi-nervous interview several years ago, I have witnessed an increasing interest in the Bible, theology, and prayer from students in my own denomination, the Presbyterian Church in America, *and* those involved in either other churches or no church at all. They've seen how the American Dream has left their parents and the Baby Boomers empty and still dreaming. Entertainment simply hasn't provided meaning or answers to the ever-wandering hearts of America's youth.

Why haven't teens who were involved in youth group in high school stayed involved with a local church after graduating? There are many possible reasons, from wanting to experience the newfound freedom of being out of the house to being intimidated about meeting a host of new people.

Whatever reasons may be offered, one thing is clear: post-high-school teens are leaving the church because they have not been nurtured and established in the faith through a Christ-centered, means-of-grace ministry. In other words, America's youth not only *need* a ministry that seeks to communicate God's grace through the teaching of the Word, the administration of the sacraments, a life of prayer, gospel-motivated ministry, and grace-centered community—they actually *want* such a ministry.

YOUTH *WANT* THE CHALLENGE

In the spring of 2010, after receiving repeated e-mails and phone calls from students about the meaning of certain words in the Greek language of the New Testament, I offered the possibility of teaching a basic Greek overview course that following summer. Hoping to attract ten to fifteen students, I knew I was being overly optimistic. But when the day came to begin, students filed into the large choir room—some of them even bringing their parents—until the place was packed! And then it hit me. These youth *want* to be challenged. They *want* to go deeper into God's Word and to mine the riches found therein. They *want* to understand why Presbyterians baptize infants and how prayer "works." They *want* to explore the development of the canon of Scripture and how to defend it at school.

This wave of interest in wanting to be challenged isn't new, but it has become a central theme in Christian ministry, thanks in part to Alex and Brett Harris's book, *Do Hard Things: A Teenage Rebellion Against Low Expectations*,[3] and their supporting website, therebelution.com. The two have begun hosting multiple conferences and seminars across the nation, attracting teens of all stripes into supporting a vision that encourages youth to take initiatives, to ask the hard questions, and to think big for God. For many, such a plea is a wake-up call from the "I'm bored" youth phenomenon we see plastered all over Facebook, Twitter, and MySpace. They are bored because they are living from one pleasure high to the next. They're not encouraged to live out, for example, the content and method of ministry service.

As I was preparing some music for youth group one evening, an early-teenage girl walked up to me and told me that she was bored. I looked up and saw scores of youth throwing the football, talking, reading, and just hanging out. I looked back at her, hoping not to be too critical. So I paused for a moment. "You know, Lauren (not her real name), the team of youth leaders is preparing dessert for tonight in the kitchen. How about you go and ask how you might serve them." Although at first she wasn't thrilled with the idea, she later told me how much she enjoyed helping our leaders and how much they appreciated her willingness. For Lauren, that was when the realization set in that she *wanted* to be a part of something greater than herself.

Poll after poll has revealed that American teenagers' number one fear is being alone. These same polls also reveal that the second greatest fear (which leads to being alone) is rejection. The irony, of course, is that these same teenagers want to be different. Youth want to be known—blemishes, sin, and all—and told, "I'm going to love you and accept you *anyway!*" If we would but realize that this is the gospel message: you are more sinful than you would ever imagine and yet, through faith in Christ, you are more accepted and loved than you could ever dream.

In March 2010, the social networking site, Facebook, became the number one most-accessed Internet site in America, toppling the web giant Google for the first time in history. Why? I contend that young people in America (who account for the largest percentage of users) are starved for truly intimate relationships. Moreover, being "accepted" as a friend does wonders in fighting their continual fear of being rejected. Virtual relationships, therefore, have done nothing but appease a God-given appetite for true, grace-centered, intimate relationships.

BEING FAITHFUL OVER BEING SUCCESSFUL

If there's anything a youth pastor knows—even after only a few months in ministry—he knows that fatigue and feelings of burnout come with the task. The constant pressure from parents, youth, the Session, the senior pastor, and family can wear a minister out very quickly. Added to these stressors come the continual expectations of these people to meet certain number standards. The most frequent question that I get as a youth pastor is, "How many?" It sometimes becomes a plague and burden—driving you to be either prideful (wow, I attracted a ton of youth tonight!) or full of despair (nobody came . . . and nobody will come next week either). It's no wonder that the average youth minister stays in one location less than 18 months![4]

Kent and Barbara Hughes, in *Liberating Ministry from the Success Syndrome*, argue that it is always better to be faithful to the Lord than successful in ministry.[5] In other words, as ministers in Christ's church, our task is to plant and water the gospel of Jesus Christ—while *God* gives the growth (1 Cor. 3:7)! It is easy to become number-driven because it makes a minister "look good" (if a lot of youth come, of course). But God's not after looks; he's after hearts.

When you realize that our task is simply to be *faithful*, you will have an overwhelming sense of freedom and joy. But this begs the question: What does it mean to be faithful to God in youth ministry? I maintain that the "how to" of being faithful in youth ministry—indeed, in all ministry— is demonstrated through the means of grace: particularly, teaching the Bible, administering the sacraments, prayer, service, and community.

Striving to be faithful rather than being successful is essentially the same as what Paul calls "boast[ing] in the Lord" (1 Cor. 1:31). Our boast should be in the work of *God* who elects, calls, justifies, adopts, sanctifies, and glorifies (cf. Rom. 8:30). Our call is to boast in his powerful working in the lives of our youth. *But he has granted his church "means" to practically boast in the Lord.*

It might be appropriate to offer a word of caution at this point. If your ministry has not been led by an emphasis on the means of grace, implementing such a ministry will likely cause some of your members, leaders, and students to stop coming. This isn't necessarily a bad thing, however. As we have seen, the lasting effects of our current youth ministry in America have left a void in churches in the twenty-somethings age group.

For some of you, this is old news and you might have picked up this book for additional support, encouragement, or an idea. If that is you, praise the Lord. But for others, this might be a new shift in how youth ministry is conducted at your church. I would suggest casting the overall vision—through speaking or writing—*before* launching a new approach to youth ministry at your church. Talk it over with your pastoral staff, your elders and deacons, or other mentors you have in ministry. Quick changes can lead to bitterness, resentment, and lack of understanding.

TOWARD A MEANS-OF-GRACE YOUTH MINISTRY

"Brian, doesn't the program-driven, pizza-party-saturated youth minister know a lot about the teenage culture in America?" Most do. In fact, youth ministries have picked up on this teenage fear of being alone and have spent countless millions trying to fix their problem. Indeed, all sorts of "communities" are popping up to create a sense of belonging among teenage Christians. However, these communities so often are formed around special interest and hobby, not the gospel. Or, perhaps a more dangerous approach, they boast of a certain moral or social justice theme as their communal bond as a *substitute* for the gospel.

In the end, however, these program-focused models of youth ministry are no different from any other social club with moral principles. Youth need the means of grace that God has provided his church to supply both the content and the method of ministry. Not only is this the biblical model given by Christ and witnessed in the early church, but it remains, I believe, the most faithful and Christ-centered approach to youth ministry today.

The following chapters will seek to provide the reader with both the *content* of the means of grace as well as how to incorporate that content into a holistic means-of-grace *methodology*. The structure will follow the historical means—Word, sacraments, and prayer—with an additional two that have been incorporated over the years under the same heading: service (ministry) and community (discipleship). I have also included a final chapter on building a youth ministry team committed to the means of grace, and how to impart this vision to them and to the church as a whole.

It is my hope and prayer that, whether you are a minister, a youth volunteer, or a parent, you will find *Giving Up Gimmicks* to be a helpful guide to starting and continuing a vibrant and spiritually rich ministry with youth.

2

WHAT IS A "MEANS-OF-GRACE" MINISTRY?

THE MUSIC STOPPED. This was the moment that I had been waiting for and, for some reason, my knees were rattling and sweat poured down my face. Directly across from me stood the most beautiful woman in the world, and I was about to pledge my love and commitment to her for the rest of my life. Was I *crazy*? Probably, but I think she was crazier for wanting to marry me!

In a wedding, the benefits and pledges of love are communicated to the spouse, and a certain level of commitment to one another is affirmed—in sickness and health, being rich or poor, in times that are better or worse. In other words, getting sick or poor doesn't throw out the commitment to love and cherish one another. Ashley and I entered into a covenant together—a committed relationship in which we both grow in our love and service to God and to each other.

Similarly, God has given the church *means* by which he communicates his steadfast, committed love and grace to his people. God uses these "means of grace" for saving his elect, nurturing their faith, and applying the benefits of Christ's redemption to their lives.

THEOLOGY OF THE MEANS OF GRACE

The Westminster Larger Catechism, Question 154, asks: "What are the outward means whereby Christ communicates to us the benefits of his mediation?" Answer: "The outward and ordinary means whereby Christ communicates to his church the benefits of his mediation are all his ordinances; especially the word, sacraments, and prayer; all of which are made effectual to the elect for their salvation." The Westminster divines agreed that Christ builds up his church in many ways including various ordinances, but they highlighted God's Word, the sacraments, and prayer.

Robert Reymond comments that these means are instruments, not of *common* grace, but of *special* grace.[1] They are made effectual in the lives of believers through God's saving, redemptive grace, and not through his common grace given to all men and women everywhere—making the sun rise on both the evil and the good (Matt. 5:45).

Reymond maintains that these means do not "work" *ex opere operato* as Roman Catholic theology contends.[2] They do not function like a magical formula of cause and effect. For example, preaching God's Word on a particular Sunday doesn't *necessarily* mean that every unbeliever who listens will surely come to saving faith nor does it mean that every believer will surely grow in his or her faith that day. Rather, our sovereign God works in and through the means of grace as he sees fit for the building up of his church.

Service and Community as Means of Grace

Through God's power and manifold wisdom, the Holy Spirit applies the work of Christ, nourishes the Christian's faith, and draws the believer into deeper communion with himself. These are the effects of the Spirit's work. But the *means* by which he accomplishes these effects are his holy ordinances, especially the Word, sacraments, and prayer.[3] This trio has traditionally been, from the sixteenth century, the bedrock of Reformed worship and ministry practice.[4] So why include ministry and community as "additional" means of grace?

While the Westminster Assembly highlighted these historical three, the divines pointed out that Christ communicates to his church the benefits of his mediation in *all* his ordinances. It is clear that Scripture affirms both service and community as means by which God nurtures and grows his church.

Jesus said to his disciples, equating service to the "least of these" with service to himself:

> For I was hungry and you gave me food, I was thirsty and you gave me drink, I was a stranger and you welcomed me, I was naked and you clothed me, I was sick and you visited me, I was in prison and you came to me (Matt. 25:35–36).

The apostle Paul writes in Ephesians 4:12 that God has given various gifts to his church, "to equip the saints for the work of ministry, for building up the body of Christ." The great example, of course, is Jesus himself, who said, "For even the Son of Man came not to be served but to serve, and to give his life as a ransom for many" (Mark 10:45). The prophet Isaiah wrote of the grace given through service by calling us to minister to the broken and the afflicted:

> If you pour yourself out for the hungry
> and satisfy the desire of the afflicted,
> then shall your light rise in the darkness
> and your gloom be as the noonday.

And the LORD will guide you continually
  and satisfy your desire in scorched places
  and make your bones strong;
and you shall be like a watered garden,
  like a spring of water,
    whose waters do not fail (Isa. 58:10–11).

God communicates grace through the means of serving each other and ministering to the brokenness of this world.

Likewise, God has established a believing community to nurture and grow faith and increase fruit in his church. Our youth at church are divided into discipleship groups (D-Groups) that meet weekly for in-depth study, sharing, prayer, and accountability. These are "safe" places where the youth can be vulnerable with each other, knowing that their true identity and security are found in Christ alone and, therefore, they can be open about their struggles with sin. They confess sin in order to find healing. They pray for each other in order to grow in their love for Jesus. And as iron sharpens iron, they exhort each other toward holy living (Prov. 27:17).

The members of the body of Christ receive gifts for the building up of the body. These gifts, Paul explains, are given by grace as a means by which God grows his church and equips her for greater ministry (Eph. 4:12). Moreover, the unity of this community of faith is the direct result of our union with Christ. Jesus prayed that the church "may all be one, just as you, Father, are in me, and I in you, that they also may be in us" (John 17:21).

God works in and through the grace-centered community of faith—the church—to communicate his grace in the gospel. We can rest in the knowledge that Jesus *will* build his church, and that the gates of hell shall not prevail against it (Matt. 16:18). What a sweet promise for those struggling with seeing immediate fruit in ministry! What a comfort for the weary pastor that the will of God for us, his people, will be accomplished *despite* our shortcomings in ministry with youth! Service and community are means of God's amazing grace to display his perfect character for his glory and our joy.

Means of Grace as a "Model" of Ministry

I sat at a Waffle House one early morning, talking with a dad who had caught his son looking at pornography. His family had just moved from a church that spent thousands of dollars creating the most spectacular show in church—complete with fog machines, strobe lights, and professional musicians writing Christian lyrics to Lady Gaga songs. Between the dueling DJs, this family was starved for the Bread of Life. When they started attending our church, they were expecting a similar story of games and entertainment, but "just not quite as much."

At that time, youth ministry at our church consisted of Sunday school, discipleship groups (with adult leaders), Tuesday Q&A sessions with me, Wednesday Youth Group, and two "events" each month. The events typically are service projects, retreats, conferences, or any number of activities. The summer program had kicked into full gear, providing the youth with Bible studies, sporting events, and mission trips.

"I just think you need more games," the dad told me across a very syrupy waffle. "If you had more games and funny skits, then my son would have come more often and not have been looking at porn." I was shocked! Here was a man who had left a church over too much entertainment, and now he wanted it back?

He was getting at the *method* of our ministry. I've learned from several encounters with parents to listen first and not get defensive, which is what I tried to do that morning at Waffle House. I even repeated back to him what I heard him say. In the end, however, I simply disagreed. Substituting gospel-focused ministry for an entertainment-driven attraction is neither safe nor right, and God has called us to so much more than that.

27

In the September 25, 2010, issue of *World* magazine, Janie Cheaney concurs that the "youth group is often seen as a way to keep kids off the streets."[5] If we can just get them into a church, that'll fix the problem. While going to church is certainly a good thing, simply going to church won't fix the problem of sin. The irony that Cheaney points out is that in an age when youth are busier than ever in sports, Scouts, math clubs, and homework, they are at the same time bored and purposeless.

This is where the importance of *method* comes to the forefront. How do we get these bored, purposeless teens into the church? Many churches have turned to competing with the world to woo them by all sorts of gimmicks and giveaways (a large church in the Atlanta area recently gave away iPods to the first one hundred youth at a lock-in!). Is that the method that God has given us to draw young people into a relationship with him?

God has called ministers and parents to supply his church with means through which he communicates grace and peace, love and forgiveness. God's Word, the administration of the sacraments, prayer, service, and grace-centered community all provide a God-glorifying and biblical method of making disciples of Jesus Christ.

At this point, you might be saying, "We do all of those things." If that is you, that's great and I sincerely hope your ministry is flourishing and that God is bringing forth fruit from your labors. If that is not true of your church or ministry, then I hope this book will at least cause you to reflect on and consider a means-of-grace approach to youth ministry. In either case, the content and method cannot be divorced.

In addition, this model of ministry cannot be separated from the overall purpose and ministry of the church. Far too often, youth ministries have become separate enclaves within a church, rather than functioning alongside and becoming an integral element of the body life of the congregation. This approach as a means-of-grace youth ministry, therefore, seeks to be integrated with the larger mission and vision of the local church—including the importance and role of families—while maintaining certain characteristics indicative of a community and fellowship of teenagers.

THE *GOSPEL* IS THE MESSAGE

That your church "teaches the Bible" doesn't necessarily mean that it teaches the *gospel*. Many confuse the gospel with moralism—being a good person, reading your Bible, or opening the door for the elderly. But the gospel is altogether different. When Jesus encountered the Pharisees and teachers of the law, he knew they had created a whole religion of works to merit righteousness. In telling the parable of the prodigal son in Luke 15, he equates his moralistic audience with the elder brother, who believed he *deserved* his father's good pleasure because of all the good things he had done.

The gospel says that you and I are incredibly sinful—more than we would ever imagine. Yet, through faith alone in Christ alone, we are accepted and loved and adopted into God's family. The wrath and anger of God have been removed, and we are called sons and daughters. By believing in the life, death, and resurrection of Christ on our behalf, we are declared righteous before God. This, of course, is the doctrine of justification, and it is at the center of the gospel message.

I recently heard a segment on a radio program called *White Horse Inn*, hosted by Michael Horton, in which a reporter had traveled to an evangelical Christian conference to ask simple questions about the Christian faith. To the question, "What is the gospel?" he received one right answer out of fifty attempts! But to the question, "What is justification?" nobody knew. And we wonder why most professing Christians describe the gospel in purely moralistic terms.

We are justified by God because our sin has been imputed or credited to the account of Christ and his righteousness has been imputed to us. On that basis—and that basis alone—God declares us "not guilty!" Again, it is not by *our* righteousness that we are accepted and loved by God, but by the righteousness of another—Jesus Christ. In the words of the hymn, "The Solid Rock":

> My hope is built on nothing less
> Than Jesus' blood and righteousness

It concludes with a powerful anthem of praise to Christ:

> When He shall come with trumpet sound,
> Oh, may I then in Him be found;
> Dressed in His righteousness alone,
> Faultless to stand before the throne

Justification should be at the core of our gospel message as we promote the means of grace in our ministry with youth. It is there that the sinner finds forgiveness and a right motivation to love, to serve, and to promote good works (Titus 3:4–9). The good works are not the basis of our acceptance before God, but the effects and fruit of our being already accepted through the merits of Jesus.

The gospel should be clearly communicated in the proclamation of the Word of God. In teaching on the fifth commandment, for example, students shouldn't just hear that they need to honor their fathers and mothers, but that when they fail to do so, they should look to God's grace and mercy in Christ Jesus, who not only paid for their sin but clothes them in his robe of righteousness. This will provide gospel motivation for honoring their parents. I remember hearing the story of David and Goliath in 1 Samuel 17 explained in a typical moralistic fashion: "go out and defeat those 'giants' in your life!" But the gospel breaks in and shows us that Jesus is the better David who has gone before us as our champion and defeated the giants of sin, Satan, and death on our behalf. Our response is to trust in *his* finished work, not our weak slingshots.

Additionally, prayer should be filled with a sense of awe and wonder as we commune with God, knowing that the only way we can approach his throne of grace in prayer is through being declared righteous before him in his Son. Otherwise, we couldn't stand before him for one second. Prayer should fill our souls with a refreshing power to display Jesus as our greatest treasure.

The Lord's Supper, likewise, should communicate gospel redemption. The invitation to come, to eat, and to drink of our Lord by faith should find its impetus in the amazing grace of God in placing our sin on the Passover Lamb and crediting us with his unblemished record.

Service and ministry are means of grace whereby God strengthens our faith in *his* sufficiency and power, not ours. During the summer of 2009, I led a youth trip to Haiti in order to give aid to an orphanage and to present the gospel. The blistering sun and heat made the ministry among the poor and sick difficult and even painful at times. But, in the middle of serving food to the hungry and sharing the gospel in remote villages, the youth were filled with an all-satisfying joy in Jesus. God was using ministry as a means of drawing them into a deeper fellowship with himself.

Most youth pastors I know have been through some season of spiritual fatigue, burnout, or general despair from believing that "my ministry is having no *real* effect." But despair meets the risen Christ. The apostle Paul, in fact, pleaded three times that Jesus would remove a "thorn" from him. Although we are not exactly sure what this burden was, it is clear that it was an ongoing struggle for Paul. His Savior's words are remarkable: "My grace is sufficient for you, for my power is made perfect in weakness" (2 Cor. 12:9). God uses ministry to communicate his message of gospel grace, demonstrated in the service of his jars of clay.

The gospel should also saturate a grace-centered community of fellowship. In a land starved of true intimate relationships, the body of Christ provides a place where real sin is offered real forgiveness. Within the community of faith, we are called to confess sin to one another and to pray for one another that we may be healed (James 5:16). Not only are we known, we are loved and accepted. That God has shown grace and mercy should give us motivation to show the same to others. Jesus—the bridegroom—has laid down his life for his bride, clothed her with his righteous garments, and is preparing her for the great supper of the Lamb.

That the Lord's Day worship service has turned into a battlefield, a "worship war"—between traditional and contemporary, between formal and seeker-sensitive—is an understatement. Too often, both sides act as the elder brother in the story of the prodigal son. On the one hand, the traditional camp will often go through the various elements of a worship service because "that's the way we've always done it." Time and again, it has turned into empty praise and external conformity instead of true, heartfelt worship and praise of our God.

On the other hand, the contemporary camp has stripped God of his power, sovereignty, and holiness and turned him into a weak but "hip" wannabe friend.[6] He's just waiting for you to stop by because he's lonely and impotent. Many times, in this context, worship becomes an emotional roller coaster where the musician builds the guitar licks one after the other until your heart breaks and tears run down your face. Monday morning, however, you are left with the same doubts, the same discouragement, and the same sense of loneliness.

Paul writes in Philippians 1:9 a prayer for the church, that their "love may abound more and more, *with knowledge*" (emphasis mine). Worship that only affects the heart and doesn't engage the mind is not worship in spirit and truth (John 4:24). John Payne, in his book, *In the Splendor of Holiness*, writes, "When Christians gather to worship God on the Lord's Day, they take part in the most meaningful, significant, and wonderful activity possible."[7] Worship according to God's Word combines the heart and mind and ushers them into an awestruck wonder of the majesty, beauty, and grace of God in Christ Jesus. This God has run out to meet us as prodigals coming home through the means of grace he has given for us to use in worship on the Lord's Day.

Indeed, God has given us means of grace, not just to reap the benefits of their content and application, but to communicate and display them as the way we should go about our ministry. These means should inform how we draw young men and women into the church—youth who are disillusioned by the gimmicks and fog of an entertainment-driven world of empty pleasure. Let us preach Christ crucified to our youth and display *him* as the all-satisfying Savior that he is.

3

MINISTRY OF THE WORD

WE LIVE IN A "FINE-PRINT" WORLD. Television, radio, Internet, and iPhones are filled with advertisements that have fine print—hoping to lure you into a bargain that is anything but cheap because there are so many costly "catches" to the offer. So much modern advertisement has targeted teenagers and has resulted in a generation of natural-born skeptics. Youth are skeptical of just about everything because the world has inadvertently trained them to be so.

In addition, news stories of pastors falling into sexual sin, secret affairs, child abuse, or double lives have been ingrained on the minds of many teenagers, making the task of earning their trust that much more difficult. The slick-looking pastor in an expensive suit telling them how they ought to live comes across as pretentious and hypocritical, whether that's the reality or not.

To make matters worse, the once-prized discipline of listening has been left in the dust by a YouTube culture of visual stimulation. Youth have traded books for videos because watching a video or a slideshow is much easier than reading a book; it doesn't take quite the mental effort. John Piper explains in *When the Darkness Will Not Lift*, "We find ourselves not energized for any great cause, but always thinking about the way to maximize our leisure and escape pressure."[1] The great irony of this is that youth are bored *because* they maximize leisure and escape pressure. The easy road of entertainment and the pursuit of the American Dream have left teens still bored and still dreaming.

More and more churches have bowed the knee to meet the demands of the visual arts in the ministry of the Word— creating all kinds of artistic backgrounds, modern paintings, and video imagery—*during* the sermon. Is there any hope for instruction from the Word in such a visual world? How can pastors and parents teach teens the Bible when everything in the world demands their attention and time? How is God's Word to be used as a means of grace in your youth ministry?

THE WORD PREACHED

Daniel Hyde argues in *Welcome to a Reformed Church* that "the chief and primary means by which the Holy Spirit communicates the grace of God to us is the preaching of the gospel."[2] Indeed, it has been argued that the Protestant Reformation in the sixteenth century was nothing but a revival and unveiling of the Word of God, and that the preaching, exposition, and application of this Word brought Luther's spark to its fruition. John Calvin writes: "The highest proof of Scripture derives in general from the fact that God in person speaks in it. . . . The Word will not find acceptance in men's hearts before it is sealed by the inward testimony of the Spirit. . . . The Word is the instrument by which the Lord dispenses the illumination of his Spirit to believers."[3]

God's Word is a means whereby God, in the first place, brings conviction upon the sinner and faith to his heart. Paul writes in Romans 10:17, "So faith comes from hearing, and hearing through the word of Christ." As much as we would like to believe that an in-depth, heart-moving testimony about a sinner's past would bring a teen to faith, it is ultimately God working through his revealed Word that saves his soul. We plant and water the gospel, but it is the Lord who gives the growth (1 Cor. 3:7).

The preached Word is also a means whereby God strengthens believers in their faith, reveals to them their sin, and calls them to rest in his amazing grace and mercy. Unfortunately, the importance of the preached Word has been reduced or neglected altogether during corporate worship. Why has this happened? Payne argues that it is "because God-centered, careful, exegetical, authoritative preaching is not appealing to the culture."[4] Success is the name of the church-growth game. Preaching, "experts" say, must go or at least be changed into a casual story time, with a few Scripture quotes sprinkled throughout.

Years ago I served in a liberal denomination as a youth pastor. I had wanted to minister in a local congregation and found myself in a semi-Reformed church. Over the previous five years, the church had experienced dissension and division (over trivial issues, of course), and the pastor decided to leave. His departure paved the way, however, for a more liberal interim pastor, who chose to preach primarily from the gospel of Luke because, he said, "it was the only truly historical book in the Bible relating to Jesus."

When I told him I was about to start a study on the book of Ruth, he gave me a surprised look. "But that's in the *Old Testament*," he told me. This wasn't news to me, but I kept listening anyway. "The youth aren't going to want to study that." He paused for a moment. "I know! You could do a series on C. S. Lewis's *Mere Christianity* or something." The truth was that the youth had *asked* me to teach from Ruth. They were starved for the gospel from the Word of God because they were not getting it during morning worship. Although I liked *Mere Christianity*, I wasn't about to let it supersede the ministry of the Word. I respectfully thanked him for his concern, but told him that the youth needed to be fed from Scripture.

The preaching of the Word should be seen as part of our worship. In reflecting on our Reformed heritage, Hughes Oliphant Old writes that, for the Reformers, "the sermon was an act of worship, the fruit of prayer, a work of God's Spirit in the body of Christ; it was the doxological witness to the grace of God in Christ."[5] The preaching of the Word is the foundational means of grace in the corporate worship of God. But what does the "preaching" of the Word entail?

To be sure, there exists a variety of opinion on the style of preaching. But all *biblical* preaching exegetes, exposits, and applies God's Word, not ours. First, the minister is called to select a passage of Scripture—preferably in a *lectio continua* format[6]—and examine the text in the original language and literary genre. Next, he is to interpret the text based on its historical and literary context, noting the original audience and the surrounding verses and chapters. This phase includes an understanding of the purpose and meaning of the selected passage. He should be careful not to take to the text his own presuppositions, but seek to know what the text means. Finally, he is to apply this meaning to the hearers of his congregation. This, no doubt, involves an awareness of cultural challenges and the immediate needs within his community.[7]

If you are a youth pastor or youth volunteer reading this, you might not be the one preaching each Sunday. However, you can build up the corporate worship of God and the hearing of his Word when you are with the youth week by week. This can be done simply by speaking highly of that time of worship or by teaching the importance of hearing God's Word preached.

THE WORD STUDIED AND TAUGHT

As a youth minister, youth worker, or parent, you may be called on to teach God's Word to youth from time to time (if not every week). You might be the lead teacher for a Sunday school, a girls' Bible study, or perhaps a large-group meeting. Whatever the case may be, it is necessary that you take time to study the Bible in order to teach accurately its truths. When you find yourself preparing a lesson, there are several things to keep in mind so as to keep the focus on the gospel.

First, pray and ask God to grant you a teachable heart. This is very important. Let his Word shape and mold your thinking—to renew your mind after the thoughts of God (Rom. 12:2). Second, read the surrounding text to get a sense of your passage's context. Third, grab an exegetical commentary that will take you into the meat of the text and will help identify the best way to interpret your passage. For example, if you are teaching on Psalm 100, a good commentary will tell you that it is part of a collection called the "Enthronement Psalms," which is Book Four of the Psalms. This is very helpful to get the overall theme. Fourth, divide up your text based on the natural flow of the passage. Remember not to force your outline onto God's Word. Sometimes, you will need to split verses up, which is perfectly acceptable since numbering of verses didn't exist until about five hundred years ago. Finally, ask yourself how this passage applies to youth today.

Throughout this whole process, be praying that God would reveal his glorious gospel in the interpretation and application of your text. Jesus made it clear that all of the Old Testament pointed to him (Luke 24:27, 44–45). He is the great Prophet, Priest, and King; the Lion from the tribe of Judah (Gen. 49:9; Rev. 5:5); and the Passover Lamb of God (1 Cor. 5:7). The second Adam (Rom. 5:14) and the son of David (Mark 10:48), Jesus now reigns as the faithful King of kings and Lord of lords (Rev. 17:14).

Let your lessons and studies drip with gospel love. Let them speak of the matchless wonder of the One who knew no sin, who became sin so that we might become the righteousness of

God (2 Cor. 5:21). Impart to your youth a kingdom vision so that they will, more and more, become strangers and pilgrims here on this earthly journey.

When I was in seminary, I began teaching youth at a local church. I quickly realized that they were much smarter than I thought. On one occasion, I started teaching through the book of Ephesians, using notes from my Greek exegesis class as my primary tool each week. Although the content of my lessons was biblical and thought out, I had little passion and love for the actual Word—and the youth knew it.

If you, as their teacher, aren't captured by the text you are about to teach, *plead* with the Lord to grant you an overwhelming joy and delight for him and his Word. Let the Scriptures convict, shape, transform, encourage, lift up, strengthen, and grab the affections of your soul. Wrestle with the Bible like Jacob wrestling with the angel, and don't let it go until you are blessed by it. If you are an ordained minister, then your primary ministry in the church is the ministry of the Word, which means that you will need to take time to prepare lessons and sermons. You will need to *establish margins* (set aside time) for study, despite the constant pressures of relational ministry.

MEDITATION AND MEMORIZATION

Robert Dabney, the nineteenth-century Southern Presbyterian and theologian, noted that the Christian should meditate on "the ascertained perfections of God, until the soul is suffused with sacred affections."[8] Two of the most intimate and soul-satisfying disciplines of the Christian life are Scripture meditation and memorization. They are also some of the hardest, which is why they have all but disappeared across the evangelical landscape.

The Psalmist writes, blessed is the man whose "delight is in the law of the LORD, and on his law he meditates day and night" (Ps. 1:2). The word for "law" may be used broadly to encompass all of God's Word. Our *delight* should be in God's holy Word to such a degree that we would *meditate* on it—day and night! Meditation is an avenue of using God's Word as a means of grace. The Psalmist goes on to describe how that grace is applied: "He is like a tree planted by streams of water that yields its fruit in its season, and its leaf does not wither" (v. 3).

Meditating on God's Word is a way that we enter into intimate communion with him and rest in his promises. Jesus said, "Abide in me, and I in you. As the branch cannot bear fruit by itself, unless it abides in the vine, neither can you, unless you abide in me" (John 15:4). It is in God's Word that we encounter the sovereign Lord, the works of God in creation and providence, and the gospel of Jesus Christ. May your ministry with youth impart a passion to say with David, "On the glorious splendor of your majesty, and on your wondrous works, I will meditate" (Ps. 145:5)!

Closely associated with meditation is Scripture memorization. Memory works like a muscle in your brain, which builds strength and makes you able to retain more, the more you exercise it in memorization. Many Christians don't attempt memorizing Scripture, and hide behind natural excuses such as, "My brain doesn't work like that," or, "Why memorize a verse when I could just look it up?"

In John Bunyan's classic, *The Pilgrim's Progress*, the main character, Christian, finds himself battling the evil dragon Apollyon. The description is worth quoting here:

> While Apollyon lifted himself up to deliver his last blow and to make a full end of this good man, Christian nimbly stretched out his hand for his sword and grabbed it, saying, "Rejoice not against me, O my enemy: when I fall, I shall rise back up." With that, Christian gave Apollyon a deadly thrust, which made the fiend fall back as one who had received a mortal wound.[9]

What is particularly striking about this story is that Christian grabs his "sword" and then *speaks* God's Word, using it as both a defensive and an offensive weapon. In Ephesians 6, Paul describes the armor of God and ends with a description of the "sword of the Spirit, which is the word of God" (v. 17). The reason this is striking is that the Greek word for "word" here is the more unusual *rhema*, which is the spoken word. In order to speak this word during battle, Christian had to first *know* the word in his heart.

It's quite amazing the number of songs we know by heart. It's even more amazing the number of songs *youth* know by heart! Yet we succumb to Satan's lie that it's of no great benefit to us to know God's Word by heart. The Psalmist writes, "I have stored up your word in my heart, that I might not sin against you" (Ps. 119:11). In an age of rampant teen pregnancies, suicides through the roof, and pornographic addictions, we still have the pride to say that hiding God's Word in our hearts is of no real benefit.

Our only hope must come from the gospel of Jesus, who three times answered the enticements of Satan in the wilderness by quoting God's Word. While we remain unfaithful to God in knowing, meditating, memorizing, and delighting in his Word, Jesus was perfectly faithful on our behalf. The good news of Jesus Christ has great application for the entertainment-saturated teenager.

EIGHT APPLICATIONS OF A WORD-BASED MINISTRY

As I mentioned earlier, the core of the gospel centers on *sola fide*, the doctrine of justification by faith alone, in which God declares us "righteous" and "not guilty" in his sight because our sin has been imputed to Christ and his righteousness imputed to us. This forensic, legal act of God's grace is of extreme importance for your youth and *the* most relevant truth in the world.

There are many ways to teach and apply the gospel and the doctrine of justification by faith alone; this cannot be denied. Understanding that the Spirit of God is the one who brings effectual change to a sinner's heart, the following are eight practical, biblical, and (I believe) God-glorifying applications of the gospel for youth ministry today.[10]

First, God uses his Word as a means of grace to comfort the guilt-laden sinner. No other truth could be so comforting than the truth that all sin—past, present, and future—has been forgiven based on the atoning death of Christ and his perfect obedience imputed to the believer. But it does not stop there. God has not just given the believer a clean slate. If that were true, we must continue to keep it clean. But God has stamped Christ's perfect righteousness on our slate so that when God looks at us, he sees us clothed in his own righteousness and, as such, we are loved as sons and daughters. For the youth who is plagued by an overwhelming sense of guilt over sin, knowing that he is declared "not guilty" and "righteous" by God brings unbelievable comfort and peace.

Second, God uses the application of his Word to convict the proud heart. His Word is like a two-edged sword (Heb. 4:12). While it brings comfort to the guilt-laden sinner, it convicts the proud-hearted Pharisee. As much as a person would love to bring his own "good" merits before God, God doesn't accept them. He calls *their* righteousness "filthy rags" (Isa. 64:6 NIV). God is pleased with nothing short of his *own* righteousness, secured by the obedient life of his Son, Jesus Christ. As much as I would love to bring my disciplined Bible-reading lifestyle, my church attendance, my kindness to the elderly, and even my success in ministry, God flat-out says that all this is not even a drop in the bucket! Teaching justification convicts the proud and brings to naught the "goodness" of self-righteous living.

Third, God uses the ministry of the Word to free the ashamed and sin-conscious youth to live a *transparent* life before

God and others. If I know that I am not only completely for-given, but that I am also counted completely righteous in God's sight, then I can be open about my sin to God and others because my salvation is not based on how good or bad I am; it's based on faith in the work of Christ on my behalf. Such a doctrine frees a person from living under the "What Would Jesus Do?" syndrome of chronic failure to live under the freeing "What Has Jesus Done?" gospel. I can confess sin to others (James 5:16) because I know that I have already been completely forgiven by God in Christ.

Fourth, God uses the means of the Word to give hope to the "failing" parent, student, employee, child, and youth pastor. Many mothers and fathers think they have failed at parenting. Indeed, many youth believe they have failed at being "good" students (although, of course, they actually might have failed their classes!). Oftentimes, children don't feel as though they can ever measure up to their parents' wishes and demands. I know of no greater hope than that our perfection is not found in being a good parent, student, or child, but in Christ who was perfect on our behalf. Jesus Christ is our righteousness. This is especially true for the youth worker. To know that our task is primarily to be *faithful* to the Lord, rather than trying to be *successful* in ministry, is to know the joy of trusting in Christ's power to save rather than our modern-day attempts at persuasion or gimmicks. Again, we plant and water the gospel; God gives the growth (1 Cor. 3:7). When we fail in some area of ministry, we must remind ourselves that our perfection, identity, or righteousness is not found in being a good youth pastor, but in Jesus alone.

Fifth, God uses the message of the gospel to give the *right motivation* for doing good works. People often accuse preach-ers who give a robust presentation of justification of holding to antinomianism. They maintain that such a doctrine leads people to abandon the doing of good works because God is so gracious and the believer is fully forgiven. This is far from the truth. This is why Paul brings about this very question in Romans 6:1–2: "Are we to continue in sin that grace may abound? By no means!" Rather than stifle our desire to do good works, justification through faith alone provides the right motivation to do them: to glorify God out of grateful love, joy, and affection.

Martin Luther was famous for preaching on good works, not as a way to earn salvation but as "a demonstration that it has been freely given."[11] Knowing that all our sin has been given to Christ and his righteousness to us, and based on that, being declared "not guilty" should make our youth exceedingly grateful and joyous. It should prompt their hearts to live out this grace-filled gospel in their relationships with others.

Sixth, God uses his Word to remind the dying of the great reward that lies ahead—sealed by the Spirit—on the basis of Christ's finished work. I tell my youth all the time that, if I am with them at their deathbeds, I wish to say, "Christ is your righteousness." Charles Hodge, in his *Systematic Theology*, affirmed the eternal consequences of the gospel: "Peace, reconciliation, and a title to eternal life. . . . The merit of Christ is entitled to the reward. And the believer, being partaker of that merit, shares in that title."[12] As one reflects over the whole of life when facing death, all of that which one calls "goodness" or "badness"; "religious" or "irreligious" comes to nothing in comparison with knowing that your reward in heaven has been secured *on your behalf.* So trust in Jesus and in his mighty work for you. The master will say, "Well done, good and faithful servant" (Matt. 25:21), because the greater Servant, the *suffering* Servant, lived and died on your behalf.

Seventh, God's unbroken union with Christ is a foundation for communion with him and with others. Today's youth take pride in their individualism, yet they are starved for intimate relationship. Their fear of loneliness and rejection finds its answer in the intimate community and fellowship of the Trinity.

Michael Horton in his book, *The Gospel-Driven Life*, makes an insightful observation about the source of Christian community. He writes, "[The church] is Christ's community—and he is the location that we all share together. . . . I still belong to other groups based on my cultural affinities, but my family is not something I choose; it is something I am chosen for."[13] Justification guarantees a relationship in which God knows everything about you—even the dirty and ugly—and loves you *anyway*. That is intimacy and the ground for real community. God knows the sin of your youth and, out of love, counts them righteous in his sight. This is how we are to treat others: "I know your sin, but I am going to love you *anyway*."

Eighth and finally, God uses his Word as a means of grace to bring himself glory. God is glorified by being satisfied in himself and enjoying his own character and work.[14] He is glorified when his perfect character is displayed perfectly, and none other could do it perfectly but himself in the person of Jesus Christ. As the image of the invisible God (Col. 1:15), Christ bought his sheep and restored the broken image lost in the fall. The second Adam was faithful where the first Adam was not. While we are covenant breakers, the Mediator of the New Covenant secures our eternal inheritance and displays God's glory by being the perfect covenant keeper. The perfect Lamb of God, slain from the foundation of the world (Rev. 13:8), was "plan A." The justifying act of God brings peace to man and glory to himself.

The ministry of the Word and the application of the gospel meet the postmodern youth at the end of his or her longings and desires. The constant desire to be free finds its answer in the freedom that Christ offers by having done all you should have done in order to earn salvation. The constant failings of morality and the constant fear of having too little faith finds its end in the One who was perfectly faithful on the believer's behalf. The gospel reminds the believer that his or her weak faith does not make Christ any *less* his or her righteousness and Savior. A believer's strong faith does not make Christ any *more* his or her righteousness and Savior. Jesus even called his disciples, "O you of little faith."

It is infinitely better to have weak faith in One who is strong than to have strong faith in something that is weak. The attempt to display moralism by being nice, good, or generally helpful to other human beings finds its end in Christ, who provides the only true *motivation* for doing what is right and pleasing to God.

4

EMPOWERED THROUGH PRAYER

I FOUND MYSELF KNEE DEEP in the Firehole River on the western side of Yellowstone National Park in Wyoming, trying my hand at fly fishing. It was one of the most beautiful days I have ever experienced. The afternoon sun cast a warm glow over the river, causing the deep blue water to sparkle and jump with radiance. Not only did the refreshingly crisp air fill my lungs, the array of colorful flowers and majestic mountains ushered me into the throne room of praise on the spectacular canvas of God's creation. What was more, my ticket for the entire trip was paid by another and I could simply enjoy sweet communion with my Maker without constantly worrying about how much everything cost.

That day in August 2004 often reminds me of the foundation and goal of prayer, especially as it relates to ministry with youth. The writer of Hebrews explains:

> Since we have confidence to enter the holy places by the blood of Jesus, by the new and living way that he opened for us through the curtain, that is, through his flesh . . . let us draw near with a true heart in full assurance of faith. (Heb. 10:19–22)

The only way I could have traveled to Yellowstone and enjoyed catching a few rainbow trout was if somebody paid my way. Similarly, it is only through the finished, paid-in-full work of Christ that we may enter with confidence into the throne room of God. We don't come to God in prayer, hoping he accepts us because of our goodness or love. We come to God in prayer because he was pleased with the goodness and love of another, his Son, Jesus Christ.

It is remarkable how prayer—real, earnest, sincere prayer—can bring treasures of grace into your youth ministry and give *you* strength to carry on. Not only does God use prayer as a means by which he works in the hearts and minds of our youth, he also transforms us as we daily commune with him in this delightful duty.

THE ASSAULT ON PRAYER

You probably remember exactly where you were on Tuesday morning, September 11, 2001. The reports and images of planes crashing into the World Trade Center sent the nation into fearful shock. If you were in ministry at the time, you probably also remember what happened the following Sunday. Churches across the country witnessed one of the largest—if not *the* largest—days of attendance in history. Services were packed with confused, frightened, and inquiring souls asking the most basic questions of life: "How could a loving God let this happen?" and "Is there really life beyond the grave?" At the same time, the president and government officials called on the nation to pray for the victims and their families.

While prayer is certainly necessary and appropriate in the midst of suffering and pain, our nation has taught teenagers over the years that we really don't need God *until* tragedy hits. America's school of prayer has educated our youth that God is nothing more than a divine bellhop.

Devoid of sovereign control over the day-to-day events in our lives, all God can do is comfort us and help us out when we experience difficulty.

The real battle, of course, is not against flesh and blood (Eph. 6:12), and Satan uses all the means at his disposal to turn the privilege of prayer into an empty ritual, without power or purpose. Willem Teellinck, the Dutch Reformer, offers great insight about the power of prayer against this unseen kingdom of darkness:

> The Lord our wise God gave all creatures . . . an incentive force to draw to themselves those things that would strengthen them. Man thus has a certain impulse in his stomach that draws him to food to strengthen him. In the same way, the Lord God has provided the soul with such an impulse toward the prayer of faith, by which we may draw the power of the almighty God into our hearts when we need strength in our spiritual battle.[1]

Too often, communing with God in prayer gets left in the dust of American pragmatism—suggesting that time at work, with family, at school, or playing golf brings more reward or productivity than time in prayer. So prayer is sifted through the "not enough time" grate. Whatever the case may be, prayer has been sidelined in the Christian life and our youth are experiencing the devastating effects.

Another danger lurking in the waters of "American religion" is prayer that seeks to subject God as a debtor to our obedience. The clearest expression of this is seen in what many have called the "health, wealth, and prosperity gospel." In this "gospel," the key focus becomes an individual's power and material reward, which is nothing short of idolatry. If you are obedient to God and are generally good, he will reward you with riches and a good life. Sickness, poverty, and the like are signs of unfaithfulness and disobedience.[2] While America offers a god who lacks power, the prosperity preachers subject God to our demands for material possessions.

What is the youth's response to all of this? David Kinnamin, president of the Barna Group, has witnessed in his research a steady decline over the last twelve years of "born again" teenagers claiming to pray at least once a day. In a generation imbued with social networking sites, he notes, "Talking with God may be losing out to Facebook."[3] Teenagers prize experience, honesty, and relationship, and our world is teaching them that those things can be found—in their purest form—from a culture of entertainment and pleasure.

The world, the flesh, and the devil have their sights set on preventing you and your youth ministry from being saturated with biblical prayer. Why? Because it is a primary means of grace by which God empowers, comforts, strengthens, sanctifies, and nurtures his people to grow in a stronger relationship with him. Through prayer, we become *strangers* in this world and imitators of Christ.

CULTIVATING A LIFE OF PRIVATE PRAYER

I had only thirty minutes until youth group began. If you've ever taught youth, you might have experienced the anxious feelings and "butterflies." Although I had studied and worked through the text I was to teach that evening, I still didn't feel prepared. All of a sudden, however, I had an incredible urge to stop and spend the remainder of my time in prayer. During that half-hour or so, I realized that this should be a model for our ministry as a whole. I'm not talking about short prayers before and after teaching, or for "traveling mercies" before going on a retreat. I'm talking about providing a venue for prayer in which every youth is not only taught how to pray, but given that opportunity regularly to pray with their peers. But the truth of the matter, I realized, was that *I* needed to live out what I professed.

Derek Prime and Alistair Begg write in *On Being a Pastor,* "Prayer is the principal expression of our relationship to God through our Lord Jesus Christ."[4] If you are going to lead your youth in a ministry of prayer, it is absolutely vital that you also enjoy a *personal* life of prayer. Prime and Begg continue: "More important than employing prayer in the course of our pastoral ministry is our using prayer as the primary privilege of our personal relationship to God."[5] As a pastor myself, I know the temptation to professionalize Christian ministry to the point that we cease to become people of prayer. True fellowship with God is often traded for passionless public clichés, which can eventually lead to paralyzing burnout.

J. C. Ryle argued that private prayer is the most important subject in practical Christianity. He writes: "Reading the Bible, keeping the Sabbath, hearing sermons, attending public worship, going to the Lord's Table,—all these are very weighty matters. But none of them are so important as private prayer."[6] Few, if any, other disciplines are more neglected today than private prayer, yet the prophets of old, Jesus himself, and the testimony of the apostles all bear witness to the necessity and centrality of prayer in a believer's life—much more so a minister!

A life of personal prayer takes a certain amount of self-discipline. If you have a family, you know well the pressures and demands (although delights!) on your time during the evenings. Even family worship and prayer together, which is a needed discipline in the home, cannot replace your private prayer life. For many people, the best part of the day to spend any considerable time with God is in the morning. It can set the course for your day with a right perspective, true contentment, and a deeper delight in God.

I usually run three times a week, not because I particularly like running, but because I know it's good for my heart and body (it's also a great way to relieve stress!). Getting into the habit of running was difficult at first, but soon it became a regular pattern and a part of the week. Similarly, a pattern of prayer can be established to build up your muscles of faith and love for Christ, and it will give you endurance in your ministry with youth.

Jesus promises spiritual blessing from private prayer. "When you pray," he says, "go into your room and shut the door and pray to your Father who is in secret. And your Father who sees in secret will reward you" (Matt. 6:6). Some of these spiritual "rewards" include having an assurance of faith, a renewed zeal for serving Christ, a reminder of God's promises in the gospel, a heavenly perspective on your present struggles, and a stronger relationship from which to draw continued strength to withstand the demands of ministry. Prayer is a gift—a means of grace—given to believers to continually experience love and fellowship with God.

THE CONTENT OF PRAYER

During youth group one evening, we broke up into smaller groups to pray for one another. A middle schooler came up to me and asked, "So what do we pray for?" The question was geared at the *content* of prayer. Such a question is certainly valid and worth considering. What makes up our prayers, and *how* should we pray?

The good news is that Jesus has given us a model prayer, "The Lord's Prayer":

> Our Father in heaven, hallowed be your name. Your kingdom come, your will be done, on earth as it is in heaven. Give us this day our daily bread, and forgive us our debts, as we also have forgiven our debtors. And lead us not into temptation, but deliver us from evil. (Matt. 6:9–13)

Some extant manuscripts add, "For yours is the kingdom and the power and the glory, forever. Amen." Jesus tells us to pray "like this" (Matt. 6:9). Jesus addresses God as "Father" and offers praise toward his holy name, that is, his character and attributes. He offers supplication, intercession, and doxology.

Supplication is simply requests made to God with a heart of faith and submission to his will. Paul writes in Philippians 4:6, "But in everything by prayer and supplication with thanksgiving let your requests be made known to God." God invites us to come to him with requests in our supplication. We are his adopted children by faith in Christ and he is our heavenly Father who desires to hear the pleas of his people. However, we must be careful to pray according to his will (1 John 5:14). This is why "prayer perfectly complements the ministry of the Word."[7] We know God's will by being in his Word, the Bible. D. G. Hart and John Muether write, "When we offer up our requests to God for things agreeable to his will, then our prayers will be a blessing to us and cause us to grow in grace."[8] Our prayers should reflect an attitude of humble submission to God's manifold wisdom and sovereign power. This is why Jesus teaches us to pray, "Your will be done" (Matt. 6:10).

He also gives us the perfect example of intercession. In John 17, before his arrest, Jesus prays on behalf of the church that they would be kept from the evil one (v. 15), that they would be sanctified in the truth (v. 17), that they may be one (v. 21), and that they may be with Jesus (v. 24). Even now, Jesus is in heaven interceding on our behalf as our Great High Priest (Heb. 7:25). Paul's letters demonstrate biblical intercession for churches (e.g., Phil. 1:3–5; 1 Thess. 1:2), and we should do the same.

One of the clearest examples of our responsibility for intercessory prayer is Paul urging Timothy that "supplications, prayers, intercessions, and thanksgivings be made for all people" (1 Tim. 2:1). Intercession for others is not only our principal mode of pastoral care, but it also provides us greater love and concern for others' spiritual and physical needs.

Likewise, prayers of thanksgiving permeate Scripture, from the calls to thankfulness in the Pentateuch (e.g., Ex. 15) and Israel's history (1 Chron. 16), to the Psalms (esp. Pss. 30; 79; 118), and throughout the New Testament (e.g., 2 Cor. 9; Eph. 1; Rev. 7). Thanking God acknowledges his sovereign benevolence upon his people for daily provisions of food and shelter, for spiritual grace, or for his work in any other circumstance of a person's life. Thanksgiving should clearly be central in our prayers to God.

To this list, the biblical authors add prayers of confession (e.g., Pss. 41; 51) and prayers of praise (e.g., Pss. 92; 145). Of all the types of prayer we find in Scripture, confession and praise have taken a back seat. Neglecting them finds root in our own pride because the world, the flesh, and the devil all seek to prevent us from admitting that we have a sin problem and prevent us from ascribing glory and praise to God. Redemptive history finds its fulfillment in the throng of heavenly worship giving praise "to him who sits on the throne and to the Lamb" (Rev. 7:10).

In total, then, we find prayers of supplication, intercession, thanksgiving, confession, and adoration. It should be noted that, as jars of clay (2 Cor. 4:7), we have a great treasure within us, the gospel of Jesus Christ. We are called temples of the Holy Spirit (1 Cor. 6:19). Sometimes we don't know how to pray or exactly what to pray for. But God's Word gives great comfort by teaching us that the "Spirit himself intercedes for us with groaning too deep for words" (Rom. 8:26). The same Holy Spirit who has been sent into our hearts, crying "Abba, Father" (Gal. 4:6), lifts those hearts up in God-glorifying, Christ-exalting prayer and worship.

LEADING A PRAYER-FILLED YOUTH MINISTRY

I want to conclude this chapter by giving some very practical ways in which you as a youth leader or parent can usher your youth and other youth leaders into this most sacred delight and duty. I also want to give you encouragement that, although prayer is not "worldly wise," it is what God has called his people to do—and our chief goal in ministry should always be faithfulness to him above worldly success. Here, then, are five practical ways to lead a prayer-filled youth ministry.

The first way may seem obvious, but praying as you start and end a time of teaching or worship is essential. Not only does this help focus minds and hearts on God, it conveys the truth that you are an instrument of the true (inner) Teacher, the Holy Spirit. This is also a great opportunity to draw in key themes of Scripture so as to teach youth the wonderful benefit of praying God's Word back to him.

Praying God's Word is one of the most exhilarating and delightful disciplines for a believer. Much praying in our day consists of talking to God and not *listening* to God. Praying God's Word is how we can "listen" to God as we commune with him in prayer. In praying Scripture, we rehearse his promises to us—"There is therefore now no condemnation for those who are in Christ Jesus" (Rom. 8:1) and the like. We also ascribe to God his attributes listed throughout the pages of Scripture. God is holy, sovereign, just, loving, gracious, merciful, faithful, all-knowing, omnipresent, good, true, omnipotent, compassionate, and more. We can also pray through the truths of the gospel with thankful hearts, that Jesus took our sin and gave us his perfect record of righteousness!

As you open youth group gatherings with prayer, it might be good simply to take a passage of Scripture, such as Psalm 23, and call the students to pray through it: "Heavenly Father, you are *my* Shepherd. And if you're my Shepherd, I shall not want anything else besides you!" When students don't know what to pray, often I'll have them pray through a psalm or a portion of the gospel of John. John 15, for example, is a wonderful passage to pray through about abiding in Jesus.

When you open a time of teaching or worship with prayer, you call attention to God's holy presence among the assembly. You can pray through his Word or for some spoken needs in your group. It is certainly appropriate to pray on behalf of earnest needs or concerns at the opening and closing of hearing God's Word taught. Sometimes, I will simply ask people to raise their hands and volunteer prayer requests if they feel comfortable doing so. I will also ask other youth leaders *and youth* (usually more mature youth) to pray for their peers. However you choose to incorporate prayer into your meeting or youth group, may it be a source of great joy and blessing in your ministry.

A second practical way to employ prayer is to break up into small prayer groups during youth group times or Sunday school. This doesn't have to be every Sunday or time you have youth group, but should be regularly scheduled. If you divide the groups by gender, they will have less distraction and can get a little more detailed about sin or life struggles. You can vary these prayer meetings by either having an adult leader present with each group or assigning an older youth or potential youth leader the task of organizing and leading his or her prayer group. This will help develop leadership within the youth group.

The great benefit to having these prayer meetings throughout the year is that it gives the students a chance to pray for the needs of others—possibly with other youth whom he or she may not know. Prayer unites Christians like nothing else. And if an unbeliever has come with a friend, youth who pray together for one another will be a great witness to the unbeliever for gospel unity. Moreover, that unbelieving student can be prayed for and cared for and drawn into fellowship in your church!

One of the best models of small-group prayer meetings is within the context of discipleship groups that meet on a weekly or bi-monthly basis. We will discuss this more in depth later (see chap. 7), but suffice it to say that meeting with the same youth to pray over a course of five or six years can be life-changing. There are countless benefits to having regular times of small-group prayer. If you serve at a smaller church where breaking into small groups is more difficult, then take the entire time to pray for each other and build up that core group of youth through this means of grace.

A third way to incorporate prayer into the life of your youth ministry is through seasons of group prayer. Two examples of this are fasting and prayer walks. At times, I will call our youth to enter a short season of fasting and prayer. The reason that we fast is to center our attention and affections on Christ Jesus, the Bread of Life (John 6:35). Jesus said, "Blessed are those who hunger and thirst for righteousness, for they shall be satisfied" (Matt. 5:6). But we don't want to simply pray and fast and not be changed through the journey. We want to see spiritual fruit spring forth from a heart of greater faith.

The prophet Isaiah writes that our fasting and prayer should lead to loving our neighbors, fighting for social justice, and caring for the poor and the outcast (Isa. 58). In this kind of giving, we are blessed. Prayer and fasting should lead to life change, which in turn satisfies the thirsty soul. Isaiah exhorts us: "If you pour yourself out for the hungry and satisfy the desire of the afflicted, then shall your light rise in the darkness and your gloom be as the noonday. And the LORD will guide you continually and satisfy your desire in scorched places" (Isa. 58:10–11).

Every time your mind thinks about your hunger, it should quickly reflect on your need for Christ as your daily bread and draw you into immediate communion with him. As mentioned earlier, prayer perfectly complements the Word. When Jesus went without food for forty days in the wilderness (Luke 4) and was tempted by Satan, he drew upon the Word of God to respond to the attacks. Fasting joins the Word and prayer into a beautiful concert. I say that fasting is a great way to do "group" prayer because fasting together can build God-glorifying camaraderie and provide grace-centered accountability.

Group prayer can also take place on prayer walks. Prayer walks can be passive or engaging. In other words, your group can simply walk through a neighborhood, your church, or a mission site and pray silently, each youth praying as he or she is led. A better approach, perhaps, may be to divide into smaller groups of three or four and simply go into restaurants, businesses, or shops and ask to pray for people. More often than not, they are open and willing for you to pray for them.

On one occasion I took three youth with me into a Subway shop. We asked the manager if we could pray for her, and she began to cry out with great relief and need. I was amazed! We stood in the middle of Subway, holding hands with this broken woman, and praying for her soul. We prayed with the mayor, with policemen at the local police department, and even with people we came across on the railroad tracks. You can have the students take turns praying for people and follow up by asking whether they are involved in a Christian community or church anywhere. Prayer walks are a great way to evangelize an area with the gospel, and doing it in groups can give greater boldness and excitement to your youth.

A fourth practical way to lead a prayer-filled youth ministry is to encourage your youth leadership to pray together regularly. Our team of youth leaders meets each week to pray for our youth, for me as their pastor, and for God to be glorified in their ministry. If you are at a church where youth volunteers are few and far between, don't worry. You're not alone! You may begin by pulling *one* semi-concerned parent along with you and slowly build a core group of praying shepherds.[9]

Finally, as a youth pastor or leader in youth ministry, you will be called to pray in times of crisis, emergency, or urgent concern. This is one of the greatest privileges and responsibilities of a youth worker. From rushing to the hospital because of an injury, to hearing of a death in the family, offering sincere and compassionate prayer on behalf of your youth is not only an example of ministry, but is actual and effective ministry. God uses prayer to accomplish his purposes in the lives of his people. It is truly a means of his grace whereby he draws us into fellowship, communion, and a deeper relationship with him. Prayer in these urgent situations *is effectual ministry*. We are to enter those times of prayer with faith-filled hearts and minds. We are to submit our wills and desires to God's and draw our youth into seeing God's Fatherly care for his children, no matter how difficult the circumstances. We are to lead them, like a shepherd, to the watering hole of God's Word and point them to the truth that "God is the strength of my heart and my portion forever" (Ps. 73:26).

We have been granted access by faith alone to the Father of mercies through the blood of the Lamb. In a culture bent on starving your youth with entertainment, lead them unto the all-satisfying Christ through the means of grace. God calls us to enter boldly into his courts of praise, to earnestly seek him in prayer, and to usher others into this most sacred delight.

5

NOURISHED IN THE SACRAMENTS

IT'S AMAZING what youth will eat. I love sushi, but it's quite different from eating a live goldfish. I sat near the back of the crowd and watched with a curious seasickness—gazing at the teenage wonder while keeping one eye on the nearest trash can! A loud, unified chant shook the entire room: "Mar-cus, Mar-cus." And down it went, to the praise of cheering youth. He was the envy of every guy and the disgust of every girl. The champion collected his prizes and walked off the stage with a "hero" notch on his belt.

"So what can we do *next* week," I thought to myself. "There's no way I can top eating a live goldfish." I was helping out with the youth program at the time, and we had been gradually escalating the "shock factor" to attract more youth. And, for all intents and purposes, it seemed to work. Every week, we saw new youth, who occasionally seemed to embody a little of the "shock factor" themselves! Over time, though, we began to run out of ideas and started getting desperate. The youth seemed bored and we had to think of something fast. We didn't have much money in our youth budget, so we decided to be good stewards and spend the rest of it on bringing a "Christian" rock band to the church (although nobody had ever heard of the group). The band arrived, set up, and did a sound check from a stage in the church gym—and topped the show with choreographed dancing. I was pumped! "The youth are going to love this," I thought out loud.

To my great horror and disbelief, only *eight* youth came. They stood lined up in a row with folded arms, listening to the thumping noise echoing around the vacant gym. I couldn't take it anymore. I was burned out of youth ministry, and I had just begun. There had to be something deeper, richer, and more satisfying than this. There had to be something that nourished the youth more than a wiggling goldfish and a high-priced band.

The absolutely amazing truth is that God has *already* supplied us with the means to nourish his people, and yet we find ourselves thinking we can do better. Along with the ministry of the Word and an empowered life of prayer, God has given us his holy tokens of love and grace—the sacraments of baptism and the Lord's Supper. But what are they and how can they nourish the souls of your youth in a regular model of ministry?

LIFE ON THE BIG SCREEN

God created us to respond to beauty and images from the beginning. From Noah's rainbow in Genesis to the conquering Lamb in Revelation, God has given us visual expressions of his character, power, and grace. Teens today are no different in being created for response to beauty. Our entertainment-driven culture has set its sights on the youth of America, offering a bright array of visual media.

According to a 2009 Nielson Company report, the average American teen spends nearly 3.5 hours a day watching television, up 6 percent from 2004.[1] That's *in addition* to other forms of media—game consoles, smart phone video players, movies, and the Internet—all vying for their time and attention. The majority of youth can give detailed answers to questions about the most recent episode of *Desperate Housewives* or *Lost*. YouTube continues to explode with instant video hits gone viral around the global community—at times drawing millions of teenage viewers overnight.

I frequently get questions from students about dating and relationships. On one occasion just before Sunday school, a girl came into the youth room glowing with high school love. "Well, you look happy," I said, already knowing that her status on Facebook had made her new relationship "official." She blushed a little. "Yeah, I'm just happy and—" she paused. "And I have a new boyfriend!" I acted surprised. "Oh really?"

It began a good discussion on dating and marriage. But one thing became clear as we talked later that day. Her idea of a dating relationship came solely from the theater. Romantic comedies (as "harmless" as you think they are) and teen-targeted flicks *showed* her what dating and "love" were all about. Like every teenage girl, she yearned for unconditional acceptance and love, and believed that desire could be met by having a boyfriend. Moreover, she later admitted that she could see herself compromising her purity simply to retain that acceptance and security.

Youth are being taught about love and relationships, abortion and sexuality, Jesus and the Christian faith, from the big screen and not from the Word of God. Because we are stimulated and energized by our entertainment and the media we take part in, television and movies have dominated the attention and affection of teenage hearts, and churches have jumped on the (so-called) bandwagon. Youth ministry in America has often tried to dovetail its programs with the luster and lure of the entertainment culture, but it simply cannot compete. Nor should it!

God has called us out of the "90210" world into a new zip code of set-apart and holy living. He provided the most spectacular visual presentation and application in the world. And it's actually the other way around: Hollywood culture has *nothing* on the joy, pleasure, truth, and experience found in God's glorious gospel—made visible and effectual through the signs and seals of his covenant of grace. The Bible calls these the sacraments of baptism and the Lord's Supper.

WHAT IS A "SACRAMENT"?

The term "sacrament" derives from Ephesians 5:32 in the Latin Vulgate, where *sacramentum* translates the Greek word *mysterion,* meaning "mystery."[2] Before the Protestant Reformation in the sixteenth century, the Roman Catholic Church recognized seven sacraments, adding: confirmation, penance, marriage, ordination, and last rites. The Reformers rejected these five on the basis that only baptism and the Lord's Supper were directly established by Jesus and directly represent Christ and his benefits.[3]

So what is a sacrament? According to the Westminster Confession of Faith, sacraments are "holy signs and seals of the covenant of grace" (27.1). They point to and seal God's promises in the gospel. John Calvin defined a sacrament as "a testimony of divine grace toward us, confirmed by an outward sign."[4] Echoing Augustine, he affirms that a sacrament is "a visible form of an invisible grace."[5] This testimony or promise of God should never be separated from the sacraments. Rather, the sacraments are to be joined to God's promises as a sort of appendix, "with the purpose of confirming and sealing the promise itself."[6] Thus, Word and sacrament are inseparably joined; the sacraments being seals of God's promises and signs of his covenant.[7]

That we call the sacraments signs and seals of God's *covenant of grace* is very important. They communicate the bound relationship we enjoy with God through faith in Christ and point to the continuity of God's progressive revelation. This covenant extends throughout the Old and New Testaments as an organic relationship that finds its fulfillment in Christ Jesus.

The biblical idea of covenant also draws our attention to the responsibilities of the parties involved to keep the obligations of that relationship. The initiator and sustainer of this bound relationship is God himself. God originally established his covenant with Adam in the garden of Eden (Gen. 2) as a covenant of *works*, making the promise of life contingent on Adam's perfect obedience. When he disobeyed God and broke this covenantal relationship (Gen. 3), death came into the world. But God extended grace and promised a coming Conqueror who, by suffering, would defeat Satan, sin, and death (Gen. 3:15). The drama unfolds and God's steadfast grace is displayed in the promise to Noah with a *sign*—a rainbow—pointing to the reality of God's promise that "never again shall all flesh be cut off by the waters of the flood" (Gen. 9:11).

In Genesis 15, God initiates a covenant with Abram. Animals were cut in two and "a smoking fire pot and a flaming torch" passed between the pieces to symbolize God's grace in paying for the wages of sin (v. 17). But like Noah, God wanted Abram to remember his covenant of grace and so gave him a bloody *sign*, circumcision (Gen. 17). Bryan Chapell explains the significance of circumcision:

> Circumcision was God's way of marking his people with a visible pledge to honor his covenant for those who expressed faith in him. Just as a seal is the pledge of its author that he will uphold his promises when described conditions are met, so circumcision was God's pledge to provide all the blessings of his covenant when the condition of faith was met.[8]

Circumcision, then, symbolized two interrelated truths. First, it conveyed the blessing that righteousness is reckoned to those of faith (cf. Gen. 15:6) and that God's people are "cut off" from all the other peoples on earth to be his treasured possession. God would be *their* God and they would be *his* people (Gen. 17:7–9). But, second, it warned Israel that she could be "cut off" from her relationship with God through transgression and disobedience.[9]

The covenant of grace is affirmed and extended in God's relationship through the biblical covenants with Moses and David, and ultimately in the blood of the new covenant, sealed by Christ himself (cf. Jer. 31:31; 1 Cor. 11:25). In the New Testament, the sign of this covenant changed from circumcision to baptism. Likewise, in instituting the Lord's Supper, Jesus took the Old Testament feast of Passover and infused it with new meaning. The sacraments are a means by which God visibly presents and applies his covenantal grace to his people.

Like the ministry of the Word and a life of prayer, the sacraments enjoy little thought or understanding in the average pew, much less among America's youth. The fundamental question we are faced with is simple: If God's promises in the gospel are true and life-changing, and if God communicates those promises and seals them in baptism and the Lord's Supper, then why have they taken such a back-seat role in the life of the church today? Even within the so-called "liturgical movement" spreading in various ecclesiastical enclaves across America, the sacraments are being diminished to mere formalism and externalism—devoid of biblical reflection of God's Word and gospel promises.

If you are a youth pastor or youth leader, you can have a profound impact on the lives of your youth by highlighting the spiritual importance of celebrating the sacraments. Not only can you teach about their meaning and institution, but you can prepare and encourage them to participate in and reflect on the life and death of Jesus through this means of grace. In such a visually charged culture, let these visible tokens of

God's grace and love transform the content and method of your life and ministry.

Baptism in Youth Ministry

I had been meeting with a seventeen-year-old boy named Mark for nearly three months. Each week, we discussed the gospel and his growing desire to be baptized. Mark wasn't a new Christian, but he never really understood the need to be baptized before. He always had very practical questions such as, "Why get baptized if it doesn't affect my salvation?" or "What's the benefit for me?"

After several months of weekly meetings, I had the privilege of baptizing him. But the questions he raised are typical of those from many youth. They often center around the *mode* of baptism—whether or not sprinkling or "dunking" is more biblical—or whether or not the Bible teaches infant baptism or believer's baptism. That these questions have caused division in the universal church is an understatement. In fact, the major denominations of the Protestant church take differing views on baptism.

I come from a Presbyterian and Reformed background, which has historically practiced the baptismal mode of sprinkling or pouring.[10] We also have historically believed that God has set apart children of believing parents as "holy" (1 Cor. 7:14) and that the promises of God are given to both believing parents and their children (Acts 2:39). Moreover, every time a "household" is present at a baptism in the New Testament, the household is baptized. There are five references to "household" baptisms, which seem to include all family members *and* children.[11] In addition, the New Testament does not give a command that children should (all of a sudden) be excluded from God's covenant family. Rather, it affirms their participation in God's covenantal relationship. The apostle Paul teaches in Colossians 2:11–12, that while the sign of the covenant changes from circumcision to baptism, the implications of the covenant do not.

Baptism, as we have said, is a sign and seal of God's covenant of grace. But a "sign" and "seal" of what? Chapell explains: "As a sign, baptism would symbolize the washing away of sin for those who trusted in Christ's sacrifice for them. As a seal, baptism would indicate the visible pledge of God that when the conditions of his covenant were met, the promised blessings would apply."[12] Baptism replaced the old covenant sign of circumcision. Paul writes in Romans 4 that Abraham "received the sign of circumcision as a seal of the righteousness that he had by faith while he was still uncircumcised" (v. 11).

Mark had come into our church from a Baptist background. During those months of meeting together, he affirmed his faith in Christ and was examined by our elders for membership. Most of his friends had already been baptized, some of them *more than once*! I told him that baptism is a once-and-for-all sign and seal because it points to the sufficiency of God's grace in his gospel, rather than our faithfulness. If baptism symbolized our need for cleansing or a renewed zeal for following God, then we should get baptized every week! But it displays the gospel visibly and seals God's promises in Christ to our hearts.

You might be asking by now how a youth pastor or leader might incorporate baptism into youth ministry. After all, this is a book on leading a means-of-grace ministry, which includes baptism. Here, then, are four specific ways to integrate baptism into your youth ministry.

First, we should *teach* the biblical significance of baptism to our youth. Many times, we assume youth know what baptism symbolizes. We assume that they understand the biblical warrant for infants being baptized. But I have found that youth have a hard time articulating the meaning of baptism. And if they don't understand what it signifies or seals, then it will be difficult for their minds and hearts to be engaged when they witness a baptism in worship. We must continually bring the meaning of baptism before them and call them to reflect on their own baptisms—that they are sealed in God's gospel promises.

A second way to incorporate baptism into your youth ministry is to continually press home the need to see this holy pledge find its fruition in *communing membership* at a local church—whether the teenager was baptized as an infant or simply hasn't become a communing member yet. According to the Barna Group, American Protestants witnessed a 22 percent drop in church attendance from 1998 to 2008 in families with children under the age of eighteen. A bigger picture revealed that, at the end of that same period, only 15 percent of American adults were members of a Protestant church.[13]

More than ever, teenagers in America are not being taught the importance of church membership. They are not being shown the need for commitment to a church body (or commitment at all!), the need for submitting to the discipline of the church, or the benefits of taking part in the overall direction of the church through voting, nominating, and/or potentially serving as an officer one day. The pledge and promise of baptism find earthly fulfillment (assuming salvation) in joining a local congregation for the purposes of availing oneself of the means of grace, of growing in faith and love for God, and of serving each other in a committed relationship. The church is called the "body" for this reason: to show that, under our sovereign Head, we function together as we live out our Christian calling on this earthly journey.

Third (and closely related to the first), we can teach that baptism is part of worship. It should be a part of Lord's Day worship because it accompanies—in a visible way—the gospel message. Through witnessing a person's baptism, we can join in the sincere celebration of God and his faithful witness to the world—demonstrated visibly in this sacrament. The promises, pledges, and sealing significance should kindle the fire of our hearts and send our solemn affections upward toward our covenant-keeping King.

Finally, the significance of baptism can permeate your free offer of the gospel to your youth.[14] Call on the Lord to create in them a pure heart, sprinkled clean by the inward baptism of the Holy Spirit (cf. Ps. 51:10; John 3:5; Gal. 3:27). Ask them to examine whether their hearts have been buried with Christ in baptism and raised to walk in newness of life (cf. Rom. 6:4). As the writer of Hebrews exhorts:

> Let us draw near with a true heart in full assurance of faith, with our hearts sprinkled clean from an evil conscience and our bodies washed with pure water. Let us hold fast the confession of our hope without wavering, for he who promised is faithful. (10:22–23)

The Lord's Supper in Youth Ministry

Around the country, "drive-in" churches boast of the option to take the Lord's Supper from your car. Pull right in, sit back, and enjoy a refreshing shot of wine and a dry wafer. You're expected to pay a small donation—a "tithe"—of course. But don't worry about your particular beliefs or any unconfessed sin. It's open to everyone because they want people to feel welcome and accepted, no matter what one's background or religious tradition may be. In the end, fencing the table is traded for curb appeal and an outdoor picnic.

Although most churches are not like this (I am thankful!), many Christians today convey a similar carelessness and triviality about taking the Lord's Supper. Youth are no different. How would they know otherwise in a culture that has thrown its importance to the back seat along with gym clothes and soda stains? Somewhere in the mist of entertaining skits and circulating strobe lights, this sacrament has been squeezed out of the teaching and worship in many churches and youth ministries.

There have traditionally been four ways of understanding the theology and implications of the Lord's Supper. It is beyond the scope and purpose of this guide to a means-of-grace youth ministry to go into great detail, but "professing" Christians have held to one of these four views. First, the Roman Catholic Church has affirmed *transubstantiation,* the idea that the elements of bread and wine actually turn into the physical body and blood of Christ. Protestants have universally rejected this belief on the basis of Christ's physical body being in heaven (Acts 1:11; Heb. 1:3) and his once-for-all sacrifice on the cross (Heb. 7:27). There is no need to continually sacrifice Jesus week by week. His work is "finished" (John 19:30). Furthermore, such a practice is seen as a worship of creation (the physical elements), which is idolatry.

A second position that some have held is *consubstantiation,* the belief that the real substance of the body and blood of Christ is present "alongside" the elements of bread and wine.[15] Again, such an understanding must be rejected based on Jesus' ascended location—in heaven—and by the necessary conclusion of eating his physical flesh and drinking his physical blood. Such a view is untenable with the biblical hermeneutic of Jesus' institution.

Others have held a *memorial* view, claiming that nothing at all happens spiritually when a person takes the elements of the Lord's Supper. Following the teachings of the Swiss Reformer, Ulrich Zwingli, the symbolic memorialist doctrine of the Lord's Supper is the dominant position within twenty-first-century evangelical Protestantism.[16] According to this understanding, Christ's words were purely symbolic and are followed by simply "remembering" the death of Christ. When Jesus said, "This is my body," he meant "This *signifies* my body." Such a view denies *any* presence of Christ in the sacrament and reduces it to a subjective act of mental commemoration.

The historical Reformed understanding, in contrast, holds to the *spiritual presence* of Christ in the sacrament. Paul is clear that, when we take the elements, we have "participation" in the body and blood of Christ (1 Cor. 10:16). The Westminster Confession of Faith states: "There is, in every sacrament, a spiritual relation, or sacramental union, between the sign and the thing signified" (27.2). In other words, the signs of bread and wine are spiritually united to Jesus. Believers partake of Christ's body and blood in a real, albeit spiritual way. We do this from a heart of faith and with the power of the Holy Spirit. The Lord's Supper builds up and nourishes the believer in his or her faith and seals our union with Christ. Indeed, the gospel message centers on this union with Christ by faith, and the Lord's Supper—as a means of God's grace—ushers us unto his banqueting table of love.

The distinction is crucial to how we take communion and how we direct our youth toward this holy ordinance. Are believers really and truly nourished and strengthened in the Lord's Supper or is it merely a time to think about the death of Jesus? I maintain that one of the key reasons why the Lord's Supper has been sidelined within youth ministries today in America is because of a memorial understanding. But if God really and truly builds up our faith and seals his gospel promises afresh upon our hearts, then the Lord's Supper should be an emphasis in what we teach, how we worship, and how we live a life of faith and repentance.

Of the many ways to incorporate the Lord's Supper into your ministry with youth, three seem necessary. First, the doctrine, theology, and application of the Lord's Supper can be taught on a regular basis. This might include teaching a series on it or simply referencing it regularly in your weekly lessons. Studying God's Word, with a heart of prayer, reveals the unfolding biblical picture of Jesus' institution of the Lord's Supper, infused into the Hebrew celebration of the Passover, and this can bring enormous benefit to the souls and hearts of our youth.

Second, the Lord's Supper can be used as a call to repentance and faith. Not long ago, I had a friend who pastors a church in Tennessee call me and tell me of an unusual but powerful true story. The previous Sunday, he had served communion at his church and, while he talked about the sacrament and fenced the table,[17] a middle-aged man stood up in the middle of the large congregation and began walking toward him. The man, weeping over his sin, couldn't hold back any longer. He had a tremendous desire to take the bread and wine after hearing of the finished work of Christ on his behalf. He received salvation that day through the preaching of the gospel, visibly portrayed in the sacrament of the Lord's Supper.

The same call can be extended to our youth. As you teach on its meaning, we hear the echo of Jesus calling heavy-laden sinners to come unto him, and his promise of spiritual rest (cf. Matt. 11:28). The struggle for youth to keep and maintain their reputation at school and with friends falls at the feet of One who gave up heavenly rights to bear our sin and experience our wounds (2 Cor. 5:21). We hear his sweet invitation to abide in him, the true vine, and find nourishment and strength for our weary souls (cf. John 15:5). We come as jars of clay—broken and sinful—to be filled with treasures of God's grace and mercy (2 Cor. 4:7).

A third practical way to bring the Lord's Supper to your youth is during times of youth worship. This can be done during a weekly worship time or on a retreat. I remember speaking one summer at a conference on the theme of "covenant." We examined the biblical story of God's steadfast love in keeping covenant with his people. As the weekend came to an end, we looked at our great covenant keeper, Jesus Christ, and his institution of the new covenant in his blood. The amazing truth about Jesus as our covenant keeper is that he was faithful to God *for us*, keeping our end of the covenant relationship.

But he also paid the penalty for our covenant *un*faithfulness by experiencing the death we should have died.

In worship, we gather as God's covenant people to offer up sacrifices of praise in the knowledge of God's truth. The Lord's Supper visibly symbolizes the gospel message and spiritually seals its promise upon our hearts by the power of the Holy Spirit. It also points us to that great day, when we gather around the marriage supper of the Lamb as a pure and spotless bride (Rev. 19:9). The sacrament of the Lord's Supper will then fade into the reality of the Lamb's celebration. May your youth be assured of their place at the heavenly table and may they be nourished in this means of grace on their heavenly journey.

6

SATISFIED BY SERVICE

IF YOU ENGAGE IN a life of self-sacrificing, gospel-motivated ministry to others, you run the risk of being filled with great joy and satisfaction. Few other expressions of faith are more central to the Christian life than being poured out in humble ministry to others, especially among the poor, the sick, and the outcast. In his manifold wisdom, God has so formed our hearts that we as his adopted children long to reflect his unmerited favor to the brokenness of this world. The irony is that while we give our hearts, minds, money, time, and strength to benefit others' needs, God fills us with grace-saturated satisfaction. *Service is a means of grace whereby God grows our faith, extends our love, and brings us joy and peace.*

I will never forget the service mind-set of a small group of Cambodian Christians, worshiping in a jungle outside Cambodia's capital, Phnom Penh. I had traveled there with a missionary team to train pastors, teach the gospel, and provide mercy ministry to the poor and sick. But my heart wasn't right. Although I liked the "adventure," my real motivation for going was not out of love for God or in gratitude for his grace in the gospel. I simply wanted others to think I was a "good" person.

Upon landing at the airport, I quickly experienced culture shock and wanted to stay as safe, comfortable, and "untouched" as possible. We arrived in the steamy jungle, and the villagers quickly swarmed around us like bees on a watermelon. The *otherness* of rotting fish, dirty children, and giant cockroaches slapped me across the face. They didn't even look like me! "Surely this was a mistake," I thought to myself.

Suddenly, a thin Cambodian man in his late twenties grabbed my hand (which made me all the more uncomfortable!) and led me to his motorcycle behind a stilted hut made of thatch and sugar-palm trees. He jumped on and, with broken English, said, "Come with," patting the seat behind him. Being a little nervous, I hesitated and squirmed with the thought of sitting right behind such a smelly and dirty man, but I didn't have a choice. I climbed on and we sped away, bumping along the dirt road until we reached an outdoor meeting house. A crowd gathered and I quickly observed that many of them were walking with wooden crutches or being carried on stretchers. Some suffered with open sores, and a cloud of flies hovered around the whole assembly. I had never seen a "church" with so many poor, outcast, sick, and needy people.

Then it hit me: *I* was the one who was poor and needy. I thought I had it all together and wanted to keep my clean little kingdom intact, but on the inside I was spiritually wanting. These Cambodian believers gave of themselves in poured-out love and service for one another. Their lives echoed our Lord Jesus who said, "For even the Son of Man came not to be served but to serve, and to give his life as a ransom for many" (Mark 10:45). That day in the hot jungle of Cambodia, I witnessed the church being the church, modeling the message of our Savior.

During the thirty-six-hour travel back home, I felt like things needed to change. My ministry with youth had been spiraling toward professionalism, a dangerous and selfish view of ministry in which the focus becomes status, money, or any number of self-centered ambitions.[1] Like many youth ministers I knew, I was using this position as a stepping stone to bigger and better things—the CEO of Money Church and free housing. I thought I *deserved* it; after all, I was doing "the Lord's work!"

On that flight from Cambodia, God granted me a grateful heart to serve him *by* serving others. He was teaching me that I needed to pick up a towel and begin washing feet. He was showing me his grace in sending his only Son, who "made himself nothing, taking the form of a servant" (Phil. 2:7). Unfortunately, our entertainment culture, our sinful flesh, and Satan are all waging war against us—telling us that *we* are the ones who should be served. *We* deserve a comfortable, easy life where everyone else must cater to our immediate desires and demands. Oh, how I pray that America would be purged from its sense of entitlement and that we would cast it at the feet of the One who laid aside all heavenly rights for our sake.

THE EFFECTS OF ENDLESS ENTERTAINMENT

According to sociologists Christian Smith and Melinda Lundquist Denton, most American teenagers believe in what they have termed "Moralistic Therapeutic Deism" (MTD).[2] Within this MTD "religion," God is a cosmic therapist and divine butler, ready to help out when needed. He exists, but isn't really part of our lives. We are supposed to be "good people," but each person must find what's right for him or her. Heaven, most teens believe, comes after a life of general good works, and we shouldn't be stifled by organized religion in which somebody tells us what we should do or what we should believe. In the end, God just wants us to try hard and be happy.[3]

MTD isn't a religion like Buddhism or Hinduism, but rather a melting-pot belief among American teenagers. Historical distinctions between denominations such as Baptists,

Presbyterians, and Methodists aren't as important to teens because they see their Christian faith as just one part of their lives like anything else—be it sports, friends, school, or family. The typical criticism goes something like, "Why can't they all just get along? Besides, aren't we supposed to just love and accept everyone and not judge others?"

In an effort to cater to this anti-distinctive trend, churches have dropped denominational labels on signs and have replaced them with terms such as "community" or "fellowship." While these are appropriate terms to convey the idea of what the church is, throwing aside distinctions can leave teens confused or uninterested in our historical heritage. Instead of holding to an honest and straightforward approach, many churches have become sneaky. Of course, they justify this as part of their "missional" outreach, not wanting to send the wrong message or to offend anybody.

One place I see it from time to time is at the barbershop. I'm usually not the chattiest individual when I go to get my hair cut. I simply like to sit, close my eyes, and let the stylist do her thing (and it's always a different woman). But inevitably, the first question asked is, "So, what do you do?" "I'm a youth pastor!" I respond, trying to anticipate her next question. More often than not, the stylist shares stories, hurts, and her lack of church attendance. I explain that I serve in a *Presbyterian* church, to which I usually hear, "Oh yeah, well, they're all basically the same anyway." I've learned that this is a trend not just with teens, but with their parents and the baby-boom generation.

There are a few key reasons why teenagers don't want to be associated with or (much less) *committed* to a church, which hinders a service-oriented mind-set. One reason is that teens have been taught by our entertainment-saturated culture, and (all too often) by their parents, to be committed to something only so long as it's popular and makes you happy. When things get hard, however, it's time to move on. Both churches and marriages have seen the devastating effects of this anti-commitment tendency. There is little wonder why "church shopping" and divorce have become the norm rather than the exception.

Second, teens don't want to be associated with a church because they are afraid of being labeled as "hypocrites." If you have worked with teens for any length of time, one thing is clear: they don't like hypocrites. In fact, most unbelievers will also tell you that the primary reason they don't attend church is that it is full of hypocrites and judgmental people. The opposite of a hypocrite is someone who is real, honest, and transparent, qualities that are highly valued among teens today. The amazing irony is that God has called us to boast in weaknesses (2 Cor. 12:9) and confess sins to one another (James 5:16), and tells us that our faith alone (not apparent *goodness*) is "counted as righteousness" (Rom. 4:5). Teens feel cheated and duped when they follow someone who says one thing, but lives a completely different life.

A third reason American youth don't want to be associated with a church is their understanding of pragmatism. "What's in it for me? God will save everyone, even if I don't believe one particular way." Teens have been taught by our entertainment culture that being good is determined generally by "what works" and particularly by "what makes me happy." Serving others is diametrically opposed to this type of thinking. So often, American teenagers' view of the Christian life is moralism, legalism, and law—not the gospel!

One evening at youth group a few years back, we had an unusually large number of unbelievers show up. I had been teaching on the beliefs of various religions and I had just begun a short series on Islam. I made a comment about the exclusivity of faith in Jesus for salvation, and a hand went up in the back of the room. "Yes," I said, "do you have a question?" He didn't agree with my statement, and "felt" that all religions were basically the same and nobody can know for sure what the truth is. I attempted to answer him there, but began to realize that he wanted to know more. I asked him to stay afterwards to talk, which he did (to my delight). The conversation quickly moved from the exclusivity of Christ to his purpose in life: "to be happy." His personal happiness was more important than truth.

Most polls today reveal that the number one goal in life among youth is to be happy. Happiness, they believe, comes from pleasure, and pleasure from entertainment. Youth pastors have picked up on this and have spent countless thousands creating an entertaining ministry: "If it's happiness they want, then let's entertain them. At least they'll come and won't be using drugs. Besides, the more youth we have, the better it makes us look!" But what's the end result? What's the fruit of a me-centered, non-service, entertainment-driven youth ministry?

One clear result is a deep sense of meaninglessness. The endless pursuit of pleasure in idolizing people and material possessions has brought with it an ever-present emptiness and dissatisfaction. Youth are easily caught up in the glamour of popularity and thrilling experience—promising satisfaction, constant delight, and joy—only to be disillusioned and confused. I once heard Ravi Zacharias, author and Christian apologist, say, "The loneliest moment in life is when you have just experienced the ultimate, and it has let you down." Like a political pendulum, the experienced "high" from drugs, premarital sex, pornography, and rampant consumerism all fail to provide rest for the restless soul. Only the gospel of Jesus Christ can call the prodigal out of the trough and satisfy his longing heart.

A second result of an entertainment-driven culture is shallow joy. In his book, *Weight of Glory*, C. S. Lewis writes,

> If we consider the unblushing promises of reward and the staggering nature of the rewards promised in the Gospels, it would seem that Our Lord finds our desires not too strong, but too weak. We are half-hearted creatures, fooling about with drink and sex and ambition when infinite joy is offered us, like an ignorant child who wants to go on making mud pies on a slum because he cannot imagine what is meant by the offer of a holiday at the sea. We are far too easily pleased.[4]

Our addiction to entertainment is a result of being too easily pleased. In other words, getting wasted or sleeping with your girlfriend has nothing on the glories of God in sending his Spirit to break our hearts of stone and give us a burning love for the King of the universe! True, lasting, deep, wonderful, and satisfying joy is found in the gospel of Jesus, not the fading fad of last weekend's romance flick.

Third, entertainment-oriented youth ministries that don't equip and lead youth in works of ministry and service fail to provide them with a biblical model of Christian living. Serving others is a means by which God pours grace into our hearts and lets us see our need of him. When we are at our end—physically, emotionally, and spiritually—we are enabled to commune with Jesus afresh and be filled with his Spirit. There is little else that restores our souls like lying down in the green pastures of Jesus' comforting presence *especially* while being poured out in humble sacrifice and service for others.

THE BACKWARDS KINGDOM: GIVING TO RECEIVE

I remember the first time I gave a Christmas present. I was probably six years old and *I* wanted to be the one to give for a change. So, I did what every broke six-year-old would do; I rummaged through the house to find something of "mine" to give to my parents. Finally, an old toy horse grabbed my attention. I took a paper grocery bag and a roll of duct tape and made something of an irregularly shaped silver ball around my gift. On Christmas morning, I could not wait to give it to my parents. All through breakfast (we usually opened gifts after breakfast) I kept telling them of how much they were going to like it, and my excitement clearly bubbled all over the dining room table, along with my orange juice. With breakfast finished and dishes washed, we opened gifts and, sure enough, they *loved* it! My joy was complete.

Jesus said, "It is more blessed to give than to receive" (Acts 20:35). The kingdom Jesus inaugurated is a "backwards kingdom," where we die to live, give to receive, and are exalted through humility. The King of kings didn't wear a crown of gold, but of thorns. Indeed, the gospel we preach is "foolishness" in the eyes of the world (1 Cor. 1:18–25). It doesn't make sense that the One against whom we sin is the very One who paid for our sin and who loves us unconditionally. Our giving of money, time, and gifts should be in response to God's grace in giving his one and only Son. Giving is a practical trust in God's sovereign care of our lives, and brings freedom, joy, and satisfaction.

Giving should characterize our leadership with youth. Jesus describes the type of leader we should be, especially as ministers in his church. In Luke 22, his disciples began arguing about who was the greatest. His response is remarkable: "Let the greatest among you become as the youngest, and the leader as one who serves" (v. 26). Jesus, the great Servant-Leader, showed us this model of ministry even up to the last days before his death. The apostle John writes,

> He laid aside his outer garments, and taking a towel, tied it around his waist. Then he poured water into a basin and began to wash the disciples' feet and to wipe them with the towel that was wrapped around him. (John 13:4–5)

During this final week before his crucifixion, Jesus continued to exemplify servant-leadership. As a youth minister, volunteer, or parent, you can provide Christ-centered leadership by serving others. Harry Reeder writes, "The Christian leader is a servant. . . . Servant leadership does not require much instruction (beyond the exhortation to be servants), but it does require motivation and humility."[5] Being a servant is exactly *opposite* of what your sinful flesh whispers in your ear. That's why it takes intentionality and gospel motivation. But, as Reeder points out, it also takes humility.

The servant heart is a humble heart. When serving, you lift others up, not yourself. It costs you time, money, and effort. *Service is humility expressed.* The great news of the gospel is that it's not about you! It never was. God has freed our hearts to serve and worship him with delight. Our lives are about serving him, not us. We are to be living sacrifices before God in how we live out gospel love with one another. Indeed, this is one way we offer our "spiritual worship" to God (Rom. 12:1).[6]

But there is also a danger in serving, seen in the biblical story of Mary and Martha (Luke 10:38–41). Martha had welcomed Jesus into her home and proceeded to bustle around the house, cleaning and serving her guest. Mary, on the other hand, simply "sat at the Lord's feet and listened to his teaching" (Luke 10:39). Luke writes that Martha was "distracted with much serving" (v. 40). From this we learn that it is very possible to be so concerned with the cleanliness of your home that you fail to enjoy time with visitors. It is also possible to serve the homeless, the poor, and the outcast, and neglect the gospel message. We must be careful not to leave the gospel in the dust of good works.

I remember talking with a prominent Christian author while I was in college at Samford University in Birmingham, Alabama. He had come to address the student body on the subject of serving the poor. During his message, he exhorted us with the familiar monastic quotation: "Preach the gospel. And if you have to, use words." He went on to qualify this quote, however, by saying that we don't even need to use words. I was shocked! Unbeknown to many in the audience, this well-respected Christian leader was advocating what is often called the "social gospel." The social gospel basically promotes doing good works without saying anything about the need for saving faith in the finished work of Christ. Being on ministry staff at the university, I had the opportunity to take him to lunch afterwards. He reaffirmed his stance, and I sat across the table wondering whether he had ever studied the Bible at all!

We never move on from the gospel. It should always inform and motivate our serving. Don't be distracted with so much serving that you neglect to sit and learn at the Lord's feet. Jesus' redemptive work should continually shape our desires to such intensity that it translates into serving action.

EQUIPPING YOUTH FOR THE WORK OF MINISTRY

"Click here to be ordained," read the caption across my computer screen. I'm not even sure how *they* (whoever they are) knew I was in ministry. Curiosity took over and I clicked away until I found myself staring at an online ordination form, telling me that I could be ordained "immediately!" No waiting, no preparation, no going under care of presbytery, and no exams! God's call on my life would be packaged and sent to my doorstep for only $19.95 (plus shipping and handling).

Unfortunately, many people are not convinced that youth pastors need to be equipped for ministry. Some even seem to deride seminary education, thinking that it's all a waste of time. Google, they figure, will explain whatever they don't know. Such a path may be appealing, but it is absolutely necessary to be trained and equipped for the work of ministry. Already, we are seeing American religion saying *nothing more* than "God loves you" because we don't know anything else to say. But these worlds collide when a youth comes up and asks, "What does it mean that God hated Esau?" All too often, the answer goes something like, "Um—well, you see, it's like God loves everybody, and um, well—"

Being equipped for ministry is different from earning a seminary degree. Like ordination certificates, seminary degrees can be bought online and shipped to your house. But being equipped takes time and effort. It takes commitment and a desire to grow in the knowledge and love of God. I have noticed a trend among pastors and youth ministers to stop reading and growing after entering the ministry. Between the phone calls, e-mails, hospital visits, and sermon preparation, they feel that they don't have time to read anymore. But if you're not learning, you're not leading! God's people want to follow a shepherd who is constantly reading, growing, listening, meditating, and doing the task of theology. They want to be given a biblical response to current trends and social issues. So often, however, these disciplines take a back seat to pragmatism and a false sense of church growth. The result is an under-equipped flock for the work of service and ministry.

Jesus knew the importance of equipping the saints for the work of ministry. A glance through the Gospels will reveal how much time he spent teaching his disciples. He could have just sent them out with no instruction and no example, but he wanted them (and us!) to understand the importance of knowing the truths of the gospel. He wanted them, by the power of the Holy Spirit, to be ready to face the challenges of ministry after he ascended into heaven. He wanted them to be poured out in service to others so that they, in turn, would become cups brimming over with the grace and joy of God.

The reason why there exist various gifts within the church, Paul explains, is "to equip the saints for the work of ministry, for building up the body of Christ" (Eph. 4:12). You have been given a gift—whether it's teaching, preaching, or evangelizing—to equip your youth for the work of ministry. So how can you as a youth pastor or youth leader, in turn, equip and lead your youth for ministry and service?

LEADING YOUTH IN THE WORK OF MINISTRY

One way to lead your youth in a ministry of service is by providing them the model of servant leadership that we looked at earlier. Servant leadership leads from the front, *inspiring* youth to join you in the vision and mission to which you call them. It shows them that you are willing to live out what you teach. It guides them in the "how-tos" of serving others with gospel motivation. This type of leadership consistently points to the grace of God in Christ and calls youth to come alongside you as you serve others.

I had the privilege of serving on a mission team in Mexico years ago with another youth group. I remember the sweat pouring down my face, making my eyes sting from salt. Everyone seemed to be struggling under the relentless July sun. But, we pressed on with the help of cool, wet rags and plenty of water, and taking breaks every so often. But I noticed that while we mixed concrete for a slab floor, the youth pastor of the group sat and watched from the shade, sipping on an ice-cold Coke. It was hard for the youth *not* to notice and, when he began barking orders to the youth, they began to resent his authority. He lasted only two more months at that church before being let go. If you want to lead your youth, inspire them by modeling what you teach, and then call them to join you in the journey.

A second way to equip and lead your youth in the work of ministry is by teaching both biblical truth and cultural awareness. Biblical truth consists of theology, historical confessions, knowledge of the Bible, and God's instructions for holy living. Biblical truth centers on the gospel of Jesus Christ and calls us to respond to that gospel with faith, humility, love, and obedience. In addition, teaching cultural awareness provides the youth the knowledge of the context in which they serve.

When I was in Haiti several years ago, I noticed all sorts of humanitarian organizations that were set up to feed the poor, care for the sick, and look after the orphans. While all these things are usually considered "good," they don't please the Lord apart from faith in Christ. Paul writes in Romans 8:8, "Those who are in the flesh cannot please God." The gospel must inform, guide, and motivate our service toward others. We must teach our youth that gospel truth should undergird our service and ministry in every culture, on every continent.

Third, we can lead our youth in service by praying *with* them and praying *for* them. As we have seen, prayer is a means by which God graciously grows our faith and draws us into greater communion with himself. When we pray with and for our youth, we guide them toward a heavenly vision of their service to others. Prayer gathers us up to see the big picture of the reason for serving, and grants us greater gratitude and humility along the way. As children of the Enlightenment, our tendency is to shed all vestiges of the unseen world. But Christ, the creator of things visible and invisible (Col. 1:16), mysteriously empowers us to serve the broken and needy of this world by his Spirit.

Finally, we can lead our youth in the work of ministry and service by serving *together*. Taking a youth into a hospice center may be difficult, but it will equip him or her for future service in similar contexts. I once took a few guys to a hospice care center in the Atlanta area. None of them had been there before and, although I explained what they might experience, they couldn't understand what I was talking about until we walked into Ms. Jefferson's room. The doctors had given her only two more weeks to live, and the sound of her breathing made us think it would be much sooner. I could tell that my guys felt uncomfortable. Seeing a dying woman ushered them to the brink of eternity. After praying with her and reading her some Scripture, we walked out and talked about the experience. As their pale faces began to regain color, I explained that we are all pilgrims passing through this earthly life, and that some are already finishing their journey. But I wanted to bring them again.

The next month we drove back to the center, and this time I asked one of the youth to pray and read Scripture for a middle-aged man. He was hesitant, but walked in anyway, prayed, and read Psalm 23 to this dying cancer patient in his forties. The guys all seemed a little more relaxed than the previous visit and felt God's presence through the whole process. Serving Christ by serving a dying cancer patient brought this youth greater joy, compassion, and satisfaction.

There are all kinds of service projects your youth can take part in around your church and community. I usually suggest that people do projects within the church body (e.g., the elderly or disabled) or the surrounding community, or team up with a local Christian relief center. Serving can be done individually, in discipleship groups, or as a large group. It can be done with parents or with friends. Whatever the case may be, it usually requires some amount of leadership to organize, teach, and guide the youth.

Another way to serve is by going on mission trips. This may seem obvious for some of you, but it is surprising how few churches participate in local and foreign missions. One of the most amazing things I hear from youth who go on mission trips is that they feel *they* are the ones who have been impacted by going—more so than those to whom they ministered! If you've been on a mission trip, you probably have experienced the same, because serving in this way is a means of God's grace whereby he grows our faith and extends our love for him and others.

Some have argued that short-term trips can actually *hurt* the people to whom youth minister. Sometimes youth will go into a foreign country without local support, do a weeklong VBS, and leave with no followup or additional contact. Moreover, many teams are not prepared to face the cultural challenges of language, customs, manners, dress, food, or style.

Steve Corbett and Brian Fikkert, in *When Helping Hurts*, suggest that short-term mission trips are to be "about 'being' and 'learning' as much as 'doing.' "[7] There should be "a training process that includes pre-trip, on-the-field, and post-trip components."[8] As of this writing, our church has been involved in a youth mission project for over twelve years to the Cherokee Indians in North Carolina. Each year, we hold a three-week pre-missions training course that requires each youth to read a book, share the gospel within a small group, and attend seminars. The teaching centers on missiology, the gospel, and cultural awareness. Practical application is solidified through break-out groups. The youth are required to attend regular meetings throughout the spring semester and a post-trip meeting a couple of weeks after we return. Such a process has been an enormous benefit in creating commitment, intentional purpose, and team unity.

If you already have a steady ministry of service in your youth program, that's great. If not, I would suggest picking up a few resources to guide you.[9] Serving others is not only a command, but a spiritual blessing and a means of God's grace. When we serve, God satisfies us with his love and stretches our faith in his daily provision for our lives. Giving and being poured out in service for others is but an echo of the sacrificial love of Jesus, who came to serve and to give his life as a ransom for many.

7

TRANSFORMED THROUGH COMMUNITY

THE IDEA OF A "YOUTH GROUP" is a relatively new concept. Over the last fifty years or so, the growth of youth groups in America can be traced proportionally to the decline and breakdown of the family. In many respects, the youth pastor is a result of the failure in the home to bring children up in the nurture and admonition of the Lord. Since our nation has become more and more secularized, there is an ever-increasing need for youth ministry in the local church.

For many teenagers today, the church is not just another place to receive biblical guidance and instruction; it is the *only* place. I remember the first time a fifteen-year-old girl named Megan came to our youth group. One of our youth had invited her the previous week and asked her simply to "check it out." The whole evening, she acted shy and seemed as though she didn't want to be there. I later found out that her parents were not believers and had often ridiculed Christianity as a sham and a manipulative organized religion. But she kept coming back, and always had more questions after each lesson. After one lesson, she came up to me and asked, "Who's Adam and Eve?" I knew we needed to start from square one.

As the weeks went by, however, Megan found a community of imperfect believers who exhibited gospel love, selfless service, and radical grace. Within six months, she received Jesus as her Lord and Savior, and immediately began witnessing to her parents. Megan's school and home didn't provide what would have been provided within the family a century ago.

The *need* for a youth ministry in a local church has also grown in relation to the growth of parachurch youth ministries springing up in schools, at parks, and even over the Internet. Para-church youth ministries have been around (in force) since 1941, when Jim Rayburn launched Young Life. Although many of these parachurch ministries see the assimilation of youth into the local church as their goal, more and more are becoming content to let their ministries simply be the "church."

The Fellowship of Christian Athletes, Young Life, and similar Christian fellowships are helpful within a *limited* area of ministry. But they cannot provide youth with the necessary means of grace that God has given his church. The foundation of these ministries cannot support weekly Bible teaching and preaching, the call and blessing of the sacraments, regular opportunity for prayer, equipping the saints for the work of ministry and service, and the privileges and responsibilities associated with church membership.

Parachurch ministries cannot conduct church discipline, nor can they provide spiritual and physical oversight by the God-given offices of elder and deacon. In addition, they often confuse youth over the importance of Lord's Day worship. If a teenager's "church" is on Tuesday morning before school, the fourth commandment soon dissolves in the petri dish of first-period chemistry. But God has graciously provided his people with a community through which he transforms our minds and hearts, and redirects our worship toward himself. That community is called the church.

TRANSFORMED BY GRACE

Theologians have often differentiated the church *visible* from the church *invisible*. The church visible includes those who engage in the life of Christian fellowship and who visibly avail themselves of the regular means of grace, although some of them may not be true believers. The visible church includes both believers and unbelievers, and the difference isn't always obvious. The unbelievers in the church may go through the motions of religious practice and duty, and may say all the right things. But in the end, they are performing and pretending as people who honor God with their lips, but have hearts that are far away (Isa. 29:13).

The church invisible, on the other hand, includes all of God's elect, in all places, throughout all ages. The church invisible has been chosen, regenerated, justified, and adopted into the family of God by grace alone. There are no unbelievers in the invisible church. The true Christian has a true faith (however small it may be) in the person and work of Christ. What is significant is that the invisible church is a community of redeemed sinners, called out by God's grace from death to life in order to be transformed by grace into the image of God's Son, Jesus Christ.

At the center of this redeemed community of believers is the gospel. The church is unlike any other community in existence. Fraternities, math clubs, service organizations, and Facebook groups all have qualified members who choose to join such communities. But those who make up the church are qualified by the merits of *another*—Jesus Christ—and elected by the sovereign grace of God almighty. Michael Horton writes, "The gospel creates its own odd community. We cannot manufacture grace; we cannot package Christ. Unlike our golden calves, it is a gift that we cannot give ourselves. God elects us for this kingdom, purchases it, and remains the sovereign chooser of the methods he will use to build it."[1] One of those methods that God has chosen to build his church is the community of faith itself. *This believing community is a means of grace whereby God confronts our sin, feeds our faith, transforms our minds, and grows our love.*

Grace is unmerited favor. It ushers the love of God to undeserving and otherwise unlovable people. Salvation comes by grace alone through faith alone in the finished work of Christ alone. Paul explains, "For by grace you have been saved through faith. And this is not your own doing; it is the gift of God" (Eph. 2:8). Indeed, God "saved us, not because of works done by us in righteousness, but according to his own mercy" (Titus 3:5). Our stony hearts are replaced with hearts of flesh (Ezek. 36:26) by the Spirit of God as a testimony to his sovereign power to bring the dead to life through the free gift of God in Christ Jesus our Lord (Rom. 6:23).

In addition to God graciously performing this divine heart transplant, he also graciously continues to complete his work to the end. "He who began a good work in you will bring it to completion at the day of Jesus Christ" (Phil. 1:6). In other words, God transforms us by grace. Bryan Chapell explains in *Holiness by Grace*, "Our holiness is not so much a matter of what we achieve as it is the grace our God provides."[2] This process of growing in grace and by grace is called *sanctification*, the dying to sin and living to Christ. While sanctification is a work of God's free grace,[3] God calls us to avail ourselves of the means God has provided to grow in that grace—his Word, prayer, the sacraments, service, and community. God is sovereign and man is responsible. Both are true. Paul writes in Philippians, "Work out your own salvation with fear and trembling, for it is God who works in you, both to will and to work for his good pleasure" (2:12–13). While the Spirit grows our faith and conforms us to the image of Christ our Lord, we are called to take responsibility by feeding in the green pasture of God's transformative grace.

The Apostles' Creed calls the church the "communion of saints." This communion involves both the vertical relationship and union with Christ and the horizontal relationship and union with fellow believers. Philip Ryken writes in his book, *The Communion of Saints*, "The communion of saints is the living fellowship of all true believers who are united in love by their union with Christ and have spiritual communion with one another as they share in corporate worship, spiritual gifts, Christian graces, material goods, and mutual edification."[4] Our union with Christ by faith provides the necessary foundation for the communion we enjoy with him and with one another. It is by grace alone that God reconciles us to himself through the finished work of his Son.

Youth need to know that it is *grace* that hems them into the communal life of fellowship with God and with one another. It was grace that brought them life and grace that will lead them to their heavenly home. The truth is that we don't deserve *any* favor or blessing from God. In fact, we deserve death, hell, and eternal damnation—the "wages of sin" (Rom. 6:23). In a culture bent on promoting an entitlement and "I deserve everything" attitude, let us give glory, praise, and worship to God, whose grace is sufficient to transform sinners into saints.

THE PRACTICE OF GOSPEL COMMUNITY

In his book, *Gospel in Life*, Timothy Keller agrees that community is the "context for change" and lists nine practices that form Christian community. We should (1) affirm one another's strengths, (2) affirm one another's equal importance in Christ, (3) affirm one another through visible affection, (4) share one another's space, goods, and time, (5) share one another's needs and problems, (6) share one another's beliefs and spirituality, (7) serve one another through accountability, (8) serve one another through forgiveness and reconciliation, and (9) serve one another's interests rather than our own.[5] The amazing thing about each of these practices is that they all promote what the apostle Paul writes in Philippians 2:4, "Let each of you look not only to his own interests, but also to the interests of others." Looking to the interests of others isn't just a call to try harder to be good, but a gospel-motivated purpose to see the transformative power of God exhibited in another person's life.

Any practice of Christian community must, in the first place, center on the gospel. If, for example, you want to serve as an accountability partner for a brother in Christ, you must be cognizant of your own sin and inability to earn any righteous merit before God. Both of you must look to the righteousness of Christ alone as the door of hope for gospel healing to take place. God's grace and forgiveness in your own life provide the right atmosphere for loving and gracious accountability for another. Any attempt to grow as a Christian apart from an understanding of the gospel is moralism and an attempt to be transformed by self-righteous dirty rags.

Gospel community is both *sound* and *safe*. By "sound," I'm talking specifically about promoting and enjoying sound theology and biblical doctrine. I'm constantly amazed by how much youth want to learn about theology, especially Reformed theology. Calvinism seems to come up every so often in secular schools in the area. Usually, the teacher's tendentious survey of Calvinism (so my youth tell me) makes jabs at Calvin and all who would consider themselves "Reformed." Youth who claim to be Calvinists or Reformed suffer ridicule and attack from teachers and classmates. The very mention of "predestination" will usually spark a hot debate. However, the polemical nature of the subject also makes it quite interesting to youth.

Sound theology begins with God's special revelation, the Bible. Any community that neglects a growing understanding of God, the nature of man, salvation, Christ, the covenant, the role of the Holy Spirit, and similar truths cannot grow in spiritual maturity. Many youth ministries have succumbed to teaching only about the latest sin at school or the most recent episode of *Lost*. Sure, they might throw in some moral takeaway, but there is no true biblical teaching. There is often no study of the attributes of God or the person and work of Christ. In the end, youth are left wanting something deeper, richer, and more satisfying than the "gospel" according to *The Lord of the Rings*.

Sound theology that centers on God in his Word will necessarily embrace the sovereignty, majesty, and power of our triune and personal God. It will behold the wonder of God's grace in drawing sinners to himself through the effectual application of the work of Christ by the Holy Spirit. It will see the purposeful atoning sacrifice of Jesus on behalf of all God's elect. It will delight in the truth that nothing and no one can snatch the Christian from Jesus' hand. In other words, sound theology is Christ-centered, God-exalting, and gospel-focused.

Part of the practice of gospel community, therefore, is savoring the glorious doctrines found in Scripture. *Sound theology leads to sound community.* It aligns our worldview with God's and renews our minds after his thoughts, not ours. It provides a framework for right thinking about how we serve, share, and affirm one another in the gospel. Don't let self-help guides to successful living rob your youth of foundational, deep, and life-changing truth.

Finally, sound theology should begin and end with doxology. Doctrine should never be separated from worship and the "so what?" question. Doctrine should inform students why they should do well in school, and how they can fight the temptation to gossip about another teen, or give them theological girth to worship in spirit and truth on the Lord's Day. Indeed, the truths of God's Word should be the lens through which they view all of life—from homework to movies, from dating to parents.

But gospel community is also a *safe* community. By "safe," I'm not talking about creating an ivory tower in isolation from the unbelieving world nor am I talking about the desire to remain untouched by the brokenness, disease, and misery of the suffering around us and among us. The safe community I'm alluding to involves the safety and security of knowing that our identity, righteousness, and acceptance are all fully secured by our union with Christ.

We can rest assured that nothing will suddenly make us spiritual orphans again. We have been bought at a price (1 Cor. 6:20), sealed by the Spirit (Eph. 1:13), and made adopted sons and daughters of God Almighty (Gal. 4:5). Absolutely *nothing* will change that! As prodigals coming home, we have been given an unwavering security in the spiritual dwelling of the Father. He has prepared the feast, set the table, and brought us into his presence where he says, "I will never leave you nor forsake you" (Heb. 13:5).

The practical outworking of this safe community, therefore, would be the absence of judgment and hypocrisy. These things cannot remain in a community that is mindful of God's grace and mercy. Paul writes in Romans 15:7, "Therefore welcome one another as Christ has welcomed you, for the glory of God."[6] Mindful of our acceptance by Christ, we accept one another with humility and grace. Youth will sometimes come up to me and tell me a "prayer request" about something they overheard someone saying. "So and so is addicted to pornography; I've been telling *everybody* to pray for him." Holy gossip is still gossip, even if it's clothed in prayer language. A safe community, on the other hand, recognizes one's own weakness and shortcomings and spurs one another on to love and good deeds. Safe community, therefore, involves trust and commitment. Commitment, then, leads to a wonderful gift of God's grace: intimacy.

INTIMACY IS THE REWARD OF COMMITMENT

If you were to go to your local coffee shop and ask the barista, "Have you been intimate with anybody lately?" he or she would probably blush and spill coffee all over you. The problem with our culture's understanding of "intimacy" is not that we value it too much, but that we value it too *little*. And youth take notice. It has been reduced to something that happens in a bedroom, rather than a relationship. But intimacy comes as the reward of commitment to one another. It is no wonder that our culture is bankrupt of intimacy in a land of broken relationships.

Commitment involves love, availability, courage, endurance, and confession of sin. Commitment shines brightest when times get hard. That's the essence of being committed to someone. That's why I've committed to my bride in sickness and in health. Commitment is seen most clearly in the light of affliction and pain. Dan Allender describes commitment as *cleaving*: "To cleave is to hold on to another for dear life."[7] One of the greatest struggles of contemporary youth culture is that they have few models of cleaving "for dear life." They haven't seen many committed relationships and, as a result, they haven't seen the beauty and reward of intimacy.

If you were to begin reading through the Psalms, you would start to pick up on a recurring phrase. In the one hundred and fifty chapters that make up the Psalter, the word *chesed* in Hebrew—"steadfast love"—is used one hundred and twenty-eight times. That's almost one occurrence per chapter! *Chesed* refers to God's loyal, steadfast, unfailing, covenant love. It's a love that won't let you go. *Chesed* is the essence of true intimacy. It sees your brokenness and sin, and says, "I'm going to love you anyway!" God's love is unfailing and unwavering, rock-solid and true. Absolutely nothing, "neither death nor life, nor angels nor rulers, nor things present nor things to come, nor powers, nor height nor depth, nor anything else in all creation, will be able to separate us from the love of God in Christ Jesus our Lord" (Rom. 8:38–39).

Youth long to be known and loved. They want to find rest in the fact that they already possess great security and hope in the loyal love of God by faith alone in Christ alone. God's steadfast love paves the way for youth to build intimate relationships because it transforms their hearts to pattern their love after God's committed love. Too often, our love is shortsighted, selfish, and a reality only as long as we remain happy. But true, intimate love for someone involves commitment.

Besides love, commitment takes being available, and being available involves being willing to sacrifice time for somebody else. Between sports, school, jobs, chemistry projects, band, yearbook, student government association, and friends, teenagers' lives seem to be more and more defined by the ability to juggle numerous balls at one time. In addition, colleges now want a full list of extracurricular activities to supplement the 4.0 GPA. In a culture starved of intimate relationships, we must be teaching our youth the importance of setting aside time to serve one another in community. Being available isn't just about sacrificing time, but fundamentally it's saying, "You are important to me and I want to serve you as we grow together in God's grace."

Third, commitment takes courage in both word and deed. I think it takes more courage to *en*courage somebody verbally than to tear the person down. It takes courage to build somebody up with words of affirmation. Keller writes, "Christians should be people who are quick to praise and celebrate what others have done, who love to praise, appreciate, and make supportive statements."[8] But commitment also involves courage in action. It means showing up regularly to church, small group, or youth group. It means listening to others with your whole self—eyes, ears, and body language. It means serving one another with yard work or helping your brother in Christ install a window. The reason that it is "courageous" is that you risk the elevation of self for another. It takes courage to be generous and selfless.

The other side of the commitment coin is endurance. They go hand-in-hand. You cannot have commitment without endurance or endurance without commitment. I ran cross country throughout middle school and high school. I wasn't a great runner and I really didn't even like running. But I loved being on a team, the community of runners all heading the same direction toward the same goal. If you know anything about cross country, you know it takes endurance. When you pass the halfway point, you either want to vomit or quit, thinking you have the whole of what you've already run ahead of you. But at that moment, you gather the strength, the resolve, and the motivation to press on—in spite of great pain and hardship. That's endurance. That's committing oneself to reaching the goal with your community.

Paul writes, "Forgetting what lies behind and straining forward to what lies ahead, I press on toward the goal for the prize of the upward call of God in Christ Jesus" (Phil. 3:13–14). The word he uses for *straining* means "to reach for" or "to stretch toward." In the community of faith, we commit to one another and stretch toward a more intimate, satisfying, and joy-filled relationship with God and with one another as we journey together toward our heavenly home. We are pilgrims passing through this earthly life, stretching toward the celestial city of God. Along the way, God graciously transforms us through the community of faith. The journey we make is a communal journey, echoing the community of the Trinity in the bond of loving peace. However, we are sinners, and running the race with sinners takes commitment and endurance.

When we fail, God has also graciously given us the gift of healing through confessing sin. Confessing sin (James 5:16) leads to greater intimacy with one another. Allender explains, "Confession acknowledges failure, but more important, it admits desire: 'I have failed you, we are divided, and I long to be restored.' Confession remembers a day of intimacy and sees the current division in light of what was once a relationship of shalom."[9]

Confession is boasting in weakness for the purpose of restoration, healing, and growth. It is a sign of trust, humility, and commitment in sharing weakness so that the power of Christ may rest upon us (2 Cor. 12:9). The reward: greater intimacy in that your sin is known and you are loved—*anyway*. This, too, takes courage and boldness. When a community of believers confesses sin to one another, that community should (at the same time) boast in the righteousness of Christ. If the Christian faith was about me keeping my slate clean of sin, there is no way in this world I would confess sin. But if it's about magnifying the work of Christ in my life, then I am free to confess sin because my sin was placed on Jesus and his righteousness was credited to my account. I rest secure in the merits of my Savior. With that freedom and joy, I now strive for a life of personal holiness.

As youth ministries across America file through one entertaining scheme after another, let your ministry with youth demonstrate a steadfast commitment to enjoying God's Word, to being faithful to him, and to being poured out in loving service to one another. The gift of such commitment is a deeper and more intimate relationship with fellow believers, which ultimately transforms our hearts for the glory of God.

GROWING TOGETHER: A MODEL OF YOUTH DISCIPLESHIP

The community of believers is a means of God's grace through which he continually and progressively transforms us into the image of his Son, Jesus Christ. Christian growth happens within the context of a believing community. In his book, *Puritan Reformed Spirituality*, Joel Beeke writes, "Growth in piety is impossible apart from the church, for piety is fostered by the communion of saints."[10] The opposite life of isolation, he later adds, will lead to the reverse. "A Christian life lived in isolation from other believers will be defective; usually such a believer will remain spiritually immature."[11] Over the years of doing youth ministry, I have witnessed few greater transformative gifts of grace than the community of small-group discipleship. In this final section, I want to give some very practical "how-tos" of organizing and growing a discipleship ministry with youth in all sizes of churches.

When forming these small groups of discipleship (D-Groups), there are some things to keep in mind:

Content

Sadly, many small groups are formed around nothing more than special interest or hobby. It might even be a good thing, like serving the poor or helping a local food pantry. Discipleship groups, on the other hand, are gospel-centered. They are chiefly concerned with growing in personal holiness out of the fact that they have positional holiness already through the righteousness of Christ. On special occasions, it might be appropriate to take the group on a service project or even have a time of food and fellowship. But the overall purpose of the group is to grow in the knowledge and love of God.

The content of the D-Group time should include a study of God's Word or some other gospel-focused lesson. Remember not to "dumb down" the content of what you are teaching. That doesn't mean you shouldn't explain the definition of justification or supralapsarianism when necessary, but don't avoid those subjects either. They want the challenge. The content should also include time for sharing—struggles, victories, fears, and failures. This fosters community growth and individual trust. In addition, time needs to be set aside for prayer with and for each other. Take the first half hour and pray for needs in the group. Bathe your time in prayer, beginning and end.

The content of your D-Group should also include loving and committed accountability. The foundation of accountability should be grace and kindness, experienced first by the grace and kindness of God. Paul writes in Romans 2:4 that it is God's kindness that leads us to repentance. Law has no power to kill sin in a believer's life. To be sure, the law is good (1 Tim. 1:8) and is a guide and pointer to that which pleases God.[12] But it is the power of the gospel, applied by the Spirit, which brings true transformation. Accountability is but a tool to put to death the sinful flesh. The English Puritan, John Owen, wrote in his book, *The Mortification of Sin*, "The choicest believers, who are assuredly freed from the condemning power of sin, ought yet to make it their business, all their days, to mortify the indwelling power of sin."[13]

We must not forget that believers have already been freed from the condemning power of sin, for it was wholly placed on Christ for our sake. Now, our task is to put to death the indwelling power of sin; and one of the greatest tools to do this is to lovingly hold one another accountable week by week during D-Group times.

Size

Ideally, you will want to keep each group between six and twelve members. This number gives the youth a sense of belonging to an actual "group" instead of simply a meeting with a friend or two. You don't want to get too large either. Each student needs that time to share, pray, and be involved. If you are in a church that has only a handful of students, then you have the privilege of having good quality time and intentional ministry with those few. Remember that Jesus chose twelve, and out of those twelve, three formed his primary "D-Group."

Dividing Groups

After working with various types of group formation, I believe the best way to divide groups is by grade and gender. For example, you could have a group of eighth-grade girls or a group of twelfth-grade guys. If you have a smaller youth group, I would suggest breaking the group into two, guys and girls. If you have a larger youth group, I would suggest having multiple "eighth-grade girls" groups. If guys and girls are together, confession of sin is much more difficult, especially sexual sin. Moreover, much more can be accomplished without having the constant distraction of trying to impress members of the opposite sex.

Time and Place

I would highly recommend meeting every week at the same time and same place. I've heard people say, "People are too busy to meet every week." What I've noticed about groups that meet monthly or even every other week is that the group becomes less and less of a priority. If a group meets each week—same time, same place—other events in their lives begin to mold around the D-Group and not the reverse. You could have it on a Tuesday or Wednesday night. Our group meets on Sunday afternoon for two hours in a corner room of the church. Other groups meet in homes. All of the groups at our church, however, meet on Sunday afternoon, which works best for family time. It's important to keep the time and place consistent so as to establish community commitment and something they can count on.

Leaders

I would highly suggest a minimum of two leaders per group. Not only does this provide necessary accountability to one another, but, if for some reason one cannot make it, the group can still meet. Larger D-Groups (with more than ten members) may need three leaders. The next chapter will be

devoted to building youth leadership, and some basic quali-
fications for those leading our youth, but suffice it to say that
great care should go into deciding who leads or co-leads ministry with youth.

Leaders should lead by example in discipleship, while
keeping their role distinct from the students as their disciples. For example, if they are going to have youth confess
sin, they should lead the way themselves. Some caution may
be necessary, however, as explaining the intricate details of
some sins can actually hinder your ministry. For instance,
detailing your lustful thoughts could lead them to lust. Or
explaining why you sometimes hate teenagers might cause
them to lose their trust in you and, therefore, damage your
ministry with them. If a leader needs help, he or she should
go to the youth pastor or senior pastor of the church. But
D-Group leaders should lead in sharing, confessing, teaching, and provide the overall direction of conversation during
the meeting.

Discipleship Evangelism

One of the pillars of the entertainment-driven model of
youth ministry is doing whatever it takes to get youth into
the church. While I'm glad youth go to church, if they don't
receive the gospel of Jesus Christ or are not offered the means
of grace, then the ministry model is doing youth a disservice.
However, most of these models of ministry realize that many
youth don't want to step into a church for fear of being judged
or for any number of reasons.

If a teenage guy comes to Sunday school or a large-group
meeting, it's possible for him to simply slip in and out without
being noticed. But what about inviting the unbeliever to a
small-group setting where he is able to share and ask questions, where he is prayed for and served. Then, when that
teen visits a larger group meeting, he knows some people his
age and grade level and they know him. The D-Group is a

good place to bring the unbelieving friend. There, he or she witnesses humility, confession, love, intimacy, and the gospel of God's grace.

In addition to these factors surrounding D-Groups, I would suggest doing what you can to integrate your youth with the older members of the church. This could be done by planning events in which the youth serve the older congregants and learn from them—their stories, their joys, and their sorrows. It could also be done by encouraging your youth to sit with other people during Lord's Day worship. The beauty of the body of Christ is that it is transgenerational, transcultural, and made up from different backgrounds, races, tribes, peoples, and languages. As much as your youth ministry might seem to form its own community (which is a wonderful blessing!), it is necessary to integrate that community within the larger community of the local church.

Christian community is a means of grace through which God transforms hearts, minds, attitudes, and worship toward himself, who is the chief end of all such devotion and worship. The communal life we enjoy is but a reflection of the *imago Dei* stamped on humanity, the roots of which are found in the community of the Father, Son, and Holy Spirit. The gradual transformation that takes place in the communion of saints will find its full expression when Christ Jesus "will transform our lowly bodies to be like his glorious body" (Phil. 3:21). From beginning to end, this triune God has called out a people for himself who will one day join in heavenly worship. I'll leave this thought with a quote from J. C. Ryle: "Yet a little while and you shall see a congregation that shall never break up, and a Sabbath that shall never end. 'The coming of our Lord Jesus Christ, and our gathering together unto Him,' shall make amends for all."[14]

8

BUILDING AND LEADING A YOUTH MINISTRY TEAM

I REACHED OUT and thrust my fingers into a shallow crevice in the cold granite. "I can do this!" I thought to myself. As I looked over my shoulder, the 3,100 feet below didn't give me great comfort, and my sausage biscuit wanted out. Meanwhile, my dad stood next to me on the rocky ledge and secured my harness. "Are you ready?"

"I think so," I said, now glancing up the two-hundred-foot rock face in front of me. "Belay," I called out.

He examined the rope leading from my harness, up the cliff, and back down to his own harness. "Belay on."

I put my foot up and found a small rocky knob on which to stand up. I yelped—"climbing!"—and quickly coughed, trying to conceal my ever-changing middle school voice.

My dad chuckled. "Climb on!"

We had taken the day to climb the rocky brow of Yonah Mountain in the Chattahoochee National Forest in the northeast corner of Georgia. Although I had been rock climbing before, I had never been so exposed, so high up, but yet so dependent on someone else. I knew that if I fell, the rope would catch me. My dad had my back, and I felt secured as I slowly made my way up the cliff.

After climbing some thirty feet, I stopped and leaned back in my harness. Again, I scanned the valley below. The view was gorgeous! The November landscape burst with bright yellow, orange, and red hardwoods—all creating a colorful contrast to the deep blue sky above. I felt so small. At the same time, I had an overwhelming feeling of excitement and joy in the adventure *and* of not being alone!

Youth ministry is similar in many ways. It's a journey, a challenge, and an adventure. But this journey isn't meant to be climbed alone. It takes people who encourage one another, who hold each other accountable, and who are constantly striving for the same vision and goal. Your ministry with youth must have a purpose or a mission. It must be committed to equipping and affirming other youth leaders in the gospel. And it must continually impart a Christ-centered, means-of-grace vision that fosters practical holiness, theological depth, and God-glorifying joy.

THE IMPORTANCE OF A TEAM-BASED YOUTH MINISTRY

Nobody likes a ball hog. Ball hogs usually seek praise from others while wearing themselves out. Not only is it poor teamwork, such a strategy usually fails to get the goal and win the game. As you engage in the practice and calling of ministry with youth, you will need others to come alongside as you lead, teach, equip, and disciple your youth. I see at least five reasons to build a team committed to youth ministry in your local church.

The first reason is that wisdom usually comes with the counsel of many. The book of Proverbs points to the need to seek advice and not ball-hog ministry. Consider some of its wisdom:

The way of a fool is right in his own eyes,
   but a wise man listens to advice. (Prov. 12:15)

Whoever walks with the wise becomes wise,
   but the companion of fools will suffer harm. (Prov. 13:20)

Without counsel plans fail,
   but with many advisers they succeed. (Prov. 15:22)

Having a team will allow you to reap the reward of others' perspectives. You might not always see the *best* way to approach a situation. When I face a challenging confrontation with a youth or a parent, I usually will call up a couple other youth leaders to seek their advice. I am grateful for the many times they have steered me away from potentially explosive situations and guided me with biblical wisdom.

Second, having a youth ministry team that makes decisions removes either the blame or the praise of just one individual. The church I serve hires two full-time youth interns each summer. A small search committee is formed in the spring, made up of adult leaders who pray, meet together, and discuss the qualities, talents, and leadership potential desired for these positions. We then read resumes, interview candidates, and choose those individuals whom we think would best serve Christ in this capacity. Besides spreading the search committee workload among a number of people, one of the great advantages of having a committee do this work is that I can tell the desired candidate, "The search committee has unanimously voted to call you here for this coming summer." Or, when I have to make the difficult phone call to tell a candidate that he or she wasn't selected, I can throw the weight of the decision on the committee: "You have great gifts and a real heart for the Lord, but the search committee has decided not to pursue you at this time for the internship position."

113

If any decision by a team or committee turns out to be unwise, no one person takes the whole blame. On the other hand, if a decision turns out to be right and produces much fruit—recognizing the Spirit's work—it decreases the chance of one individual receiving the glory. A team, however, can be commended as they give praise to God for what he has done through their ministry together.

A third reason to build a youth ministry team is for mutual accountability and encouragement. Each week, I meet with a fellow youth leader who also happens to be an elder at our church. We talk through personal purity, family issues, and our ministry with youth. We hold each other accountable by asking questions and following up with personal struggles if needed. We also encourage one another to press on when times get tough. When I see little spiritual fruit on a Sunday morning among the youth, he tells me to keep going—to strive for faithfulness and let the Lord work his grace in their lives. He reminds me that it takes time and that sanctification is a process. He leads a D-Group, and I try to encourage him not to give up on "his guys" and to lead them with brokenness and humility. Being part of a team also encourages each team member with a sense of a greater purpose and vision for what they are doing individually.

Fourth, a youth team can have a greater impact and ministry than an individual. Jesus was the perfect example of this. He chose twelve men to train and disciple. He then sent them out to do the work of ministry (Matt. 10:5). While he could have done the work of the church without his disciples, Jesus chose to include them in the joy of gospel ministry. After his ascension, his Spirit continued to guide the disciples, and to empower them as they led the early church. They traveled all over, preaching and teaching the good news of Jesus Christ.

Such a team-based ministry can be as simple as having a trained adult find three students to love and disciple, and then following up with that individual. You could ask him or her then to find another co-leader who will join them in ministry. Eventually, as their group grows, they might need to split into two groups, each taking a group. Having a youth ministry team will allow a church to have a greater ministry impact on more youth than a single individual.

A final reason to build a team is that, in the possibility of a youth minister or leader leaving the church (for any number of reasons), the youth program doesn't crumble. I've seen youth pastors build up ministry empires around themselves, their personalities, or their unique styles. But if and when one of these youth leaders leaves the church, nobody is equipped or ready to sustain the level of ministry. The result is usually chaos, confusion, and youth looking for another place to grow.

I probably need to clarify the specific structure of a youth ministry team. To be sure, there are many types of "teams" in a local church. For example, it is necessary to involve parents in your ministry with youth. They need to be constant sources of information, support, and counsel. They also need to know that you trust them and listen to their advice. Remember that *they*—not you—are the greatest influences in their children's lives.

Team support also comes from staff, the Session, the diaconate, and the youth themselves. One of the best things you can do with your youth is to build up the other ministries, staff, and officers in your church. This communicates to them that you are all on the same team. Equally important is it to build up the youth pastor(s) before you.[1] I have seen new youth ministers come into a church, change the whole program, and make any current leaders go "their way or the highway." This creates bitterness and resentment, and breaks unity in the church. If these changes need to be made, then make them gradually, unless something is unbiblical. This shows that you care for others, that you're willing to listen, and that you work as a team player.

The officers of the church are also vital to youth ministry. They should continually be informed about what's happening, how they should pray and shepherd the families of your youth, and be involved in the overall purpose and vision of your ministry. It would be wise to select some representatives on the Session and diaconate who can speak for the ministry. Creating an entirely separate community of youth within the church is neither right nor safe. Although a certain community does need to be established, that community should always be integrated into the church body as a whole.

While all of these are supporting "teams" for ministry, the team that I am specifically suggesting in this chapter is made up of recruited, equipped, and affirmed adults who love God and love youth. They make up your core group of leaders who work on a regular basis with teens in your church.

RECRUITING, EQUIPPING, AND AFFIRMING YOUTH LEADERS

Recruiting, equipping, and affirming youth leaders do not come easily for most people. It takes intentionality, hard work, planning, and courage. But all three are essential to building a youth team that is energized for sustained ministry.

Recruiting

In talking with youth pastors in my own denomination, I have realized how difficult it can be to recruit volunteers to work with youth. Many adults are terrified to walk into a room full of out-of-control teenagers, or they feel like they have absolutely nothing in common with the iPod, Twitter, YouTube generation. Even if you ask them in the most upbeat, encouraging manner—"Hey, you wanna volunteer with youth?"—they look at you like they have just seen a ghost. So how do you build a team if it seems as though adults run for the hills when you mention the need?

It might seem obvious, but many youth pastors and youth leaders don't have youth teams simply because they don't *ask*. Asking is a great place to start. Identify a potential leader, pray about the person, and then ask whether he or she would be willing to serve. Give prospective leaders confidence that they won't go it alone and that they will be equipped to do their task well. Perhaps you only need to ask them to "consider" the possibility, and either have them get back with you or let them know that you will get back with them in a week.

A second way to recruit is to change your whole mind-set about a youth volunteer. For example, I never call my adult youth volunteers, "volunteers." That reduces their ministry to impersonal work, a sacrifice of time, and vision*less* responsibility. Rather, I like to call them "youth shepherds." Unlike the term "volunteer," "youth shepherd" refers more to calling and purpose. In other words, *it is crucial to show them vision before need.* A shepherd watches over a flock, feeds the flock, challenges the flock, confronts the flock, and leads the flock to the green pastures of God's transformative grace.

However, I need to offer a word of caution. Although it is tempting to have anybody who wants to work with youth join you, it's not always a good idea. Just because somebody *wants* to work with youth doesn't mean that person *should* work with youth. Just because he or she is a talented communicator, or funny, or possesses a PhD doesn't make the person qualified to lead in the youth ministry. Before you let people work with youth, get to know them. Meet with them and ask hard questions about their personal lives and habits. Ask about their hobbies, what they like to do on weekends, and their availability to work with youth. Ask about their understanding of the gospel. You need to make sure, too, that they are willing to submit to your authority and work as a team player.

Recruiting can take place from the pulpit before worship on the Lord's Day or by writing an e-mail or letter. But whatever mode you use to recruit, make sure you have a clear understanding of the eternal impact an adult leader can have in a teenager's life. This will inform what you say and how you say it.

Equipping

Each summer, I lead a weekend retreat for current and potential youth shepherds. Only adults are invited, and it's one of my favorite times of the year! We get away in order to take extended and focused time looking at the previous year's ministry, planning for the following year, and discussing the overall goal of youth ministry at our church. We try to identify what went well, what didn't, and what might need to change. I also try to teach and equip them with a passion for working with teens by showing them a vision of a gospel-driven, Christ-centered ministry that incorporates the means of grace.

Our youth shepherds also sign a one-year commitment to serve with youth in one of five ways: (1) they can be a D-Group leader or co-leader; (2) they can serve as a "ministry of presence," where they simply come to youth events or Sunday school; (3) they can sign up to shepherd retreats and special events; (4) they can serve by doing manual labor in setting up tables, chairs, etc.; or (5) they can help me in one-on-one mentoring with students who need a little more focused discipleship. This commitment is necessary and provides a reminder to them of their calling. It also shows the youth that their leaders care and are committed to seeing them grow in the knowledge and love of Jesus, through thick and thin.

Equipping leaders also means inspiring them by your own example. Be willing to be transparent and vulnerable with them about your struggles as well as your love for Christ. Teach them how to have regular personal devotions or how to grow in their own relationship with God. Teach them through lessons, letters, e-mails, and conversations about how the gospel relates to them and their youth. Pray with and for them. Have them partake in the Lord's Supper regularly. Allow them to come with you as you serve the homeless and the outcast. Invite them to be involved in your small group of adults to study together, pray together, and live out the Christian faith together. All of these means of grace equip and build up a youth ministry team.

Affirming

Along with recruiting and equipping, youth shepherds/ leaders need to be constantly affirmed in their ministry calling and practice. Satan is the great accuser, and seeks to cast doubt and despair into the minds and hearts of the faithful. You must be on guard and combat his schemes by pointing your leaders to the gospel over and over again. They are to look unto Christ, the founder and perfecter of their faith (Heb. 12:2), for their righteous standing and atoning sacrifice. Remind them of their status as adopted sons and daughters of God almighty, a status that can never be taken away. I've had youth shepherds come up to me and say, "Brian, I don't feel worthy enough to lead the youth." To which I respond, "You shouldn't, but God has declared you worthy in his sight and given you the tools and power to press on."

You can also affirm youth leaders by listening to them. This may seem elementary, but you never outgrow the need to listen. It communicates a desire to work as a team, your heart for them, and humility. Along with e-mails, handwritten personal letters are of enormous value. I would avoid printed cards, and simply take out a sheet of paper and go to work. Giving small gifts such as good books every so often also builds them up, gives them something to grow in, and affirms them in their calling and work with youth.

Finally, I would suggest that you lovingly challenge them. You might be wondering how challenging a person can be affirming, but it can actually be one of the greatest witnesses to true concern and love for another. I once saw a banner tied in front of a church during its mission week that read, "They don't care about how much you know until they know how much you care." That is not only true of your ministry with youth, but also true of your ministry with your youth *leaders*. If they know that you care for them, they will follow you and be receptive to constructive criticism. The result is their being affirmed in their calling and ministry practice. Building a youth ministry team takes patience and compassion. But it also takes persistence in imparting a purpose and vision for your ministry.

ESTABLISHING A PURPOSE FOR YOUTH MINISTRY

The purpose of any ministry, any church, and all worship is the glory of God. How do you lead a youth ministry, then, that has the glory of God as its overarching purpose? Doug Fields lists five core purposes for building a youth program: evangelism, worship, fellowship, discipleship, and ministry.[2] But what I'm talking about is one step further. On the one hand, you can have entertaining evangelism, entertaining worship, entertaining fellowship, and so on. Not all entertainment is wrong. What is wrong is a ministry *driven* by entertainment. But on the other hand, you can have ministries of evangelism, worship, fellowship, discipleship, and ministry that find greater purpose in displaying the glory of God in the gospel of Jesus Christ. How you go about these five purposes that Fields mentions gets at the heart of the greater purpose of your youth ministry.

Leading a ministry without purpose is like sailing with a rudderless boat. You are at the mercy of every wind, every fad, and every trend that blows your way. But a purpose steadies your course and continually calls you ahead toward the glory of God. It sets your sight on a vision—making disciples of Jesus Christ—and steers all the working parts to reach that destination. Having a purpose unites your team and calls others to join you in the journey.

A couple of years ago, I sat down with another youth shepherd and hammered out a new purpose statement for our youth ministry:

> To glorify God by treasuring him above all things, by creating a transparent and grace-centered community of fellowship, by participating in the expansion of Christ's kingdom, and by encouraging spiritual growth through the teaching of God's Word, worship, service, and prayer.

We wanted to recognize the glory of God as our chief end, and we also wanted to write down how we would practically steer the ship toward that purpose. If you do not currently have a purpose in your youth ministry, I would strongly suggest working out one that you can get behind with your heart, mind, soul, and strength. Then, ask yourself whether every program, event, retreat, or lesson that is a part of your ministry can support that overall purpose. If not, throw it out or transform it so that it does.

Establishing a purpose for your ministry builds a teamwork mentality because it points others toward something greater than one person. Having a purpose also allows adults—who would otherwise be terrified of working with youth—something

121

to aim for. It gets their mind off their own shortcomings and directs them toward a gospel goal.

God's Word, prayer, the sacraments, service, and community all provide support for a purposeful youth ministry. Let these shape the content of your message as well as the method of your ministry. Let these, not entertainment, communicate Christ to the lives of your youth. Let these steer the course of your ministry and give you great joy and confidence.

IMPARTING A VISION OF A MEANS-OF-GRACE MINISTRY

Jesus said, "I am the vine; you are the branches. Whoever abides in me and I in him, he it is that bears much fruit, for apart from me you can do nothing" (John 15:5). Apart from the Spirit taking the finished work of Christ and applying it to our lives, we can do *nothing* that would please or honor God. Here, Jesus calls us to a singular calling and focus: "abide in me." As youth workers, our task is to guide youth to the true Vine, where they will find grace, salvation, and the lordship of Christ. The means of grace are instruments and gifts that God has given his church for the increase of faith, hope, love, and joy in him. Youth ministry should always direct youth toward God, not man. It should always concern itself with bearing fruit as an effect of abiding in the Vine.

As we conclude, I want to provide five takeaways from a means-of-grace model of youth ministry. They are big-picture practices of gospel-rich ministry that will give you great freedom and joy as you labor among America's youth. First, let the Word of Christ dwell in you richly (Col. 3:16) and shape your overall ministry with youth. Let your ministry be characterized by the teaching of the Bible. Nothing should substitute for God's Word in a gospel-rich youth ministry. It must remain central to community life, to youth events, to retreats, to Sunday school, and to your own growth in grace. It is a lamp unto our feet and a light unto our path (Ps. 119:105). The Word of

God is a means by which he graciously shapes our thinking, confronts our sin, and revives our weary souls.

Second, cultivate a life of prayer that permeates your ministry with youth. Lead by example and inspire them to establish regular patterns of prayer throughout the week. Teach them how to pray with an understanding of God's sovereignty and how he has ordained prayer as the means by which he works in his creation. Prayer unites mind and heart into the bosom of the Father—finding rest, power, and wisdom for the day. Prayer is a means by which God graciously draws us into deeper fellowship with him and conforms our wills to his.

A third take-away from a means-of-grace ministry is to provide regular opportunities of partaking in the Lord's Supper. If certain youth are not yet communing members of your church, but profess faith in Christ, then encourage them take the steps to become members. In the Lord's Supper, God mysteriously imparts grace and nourishment for believing souls. He graciously draws us back to our first love (Rev. 2:4), to the One who was wounded for our transgressions and crushed for our iniquities (Isa. 53:5). In it, he reminds us of our great sin *and* our great Savior. Death has been swallowed up in victory (1 Cor. 15:54)! The Lord's Supper is a means whereby God graciously calls us to repentance and faith in the Lamb who was slain.

Fourthly, equip youth and lead them in the work of service and ministry. In a culture bent on self-centered pleasure and entertainment, devoid of satisfying joy, and broken by the boredom of an insatiable desire for more, *serve* others out of a gospel-motivated heart for the glory of God in Christ Jesus. The One who came, not to be served, but to serve and to give his life as a ransom for many (Mk. 10:45) calls you to be his hands and feet to a lost and broken world. Moreover, he calls you to be his herald in proclaiming the good news of the gospel. Service and ministry are means by which God

123

graciously grows our faith, extends our love, and brings us joy, satisfaction, and peace.

Finally, strive to provide a transformative community that is shaped by the gospel, committed to one another, sound in theology, and safe in practice. Lead with a sense of brokenness, allowing the power of Christ to rest upon you (2 Cor. 12:9). Risk being vulnerable with one another in order "to grow up in every way into him who is the head, into Christ" (Eph. 4:15). Strive for personal holiness and gospel unity, to be *one* even as the Son and the Father are one (John 17:21). Let intimate relationships spring forth as the reward of commitment with one another. Relish in the grace and beauty of being known and loved at the same time. Foster an encouraging spirit among your youth that establishes humility and selflessness. And provide them a ministry of sustained discipleship, looking to God who not only began his miraculous work in them, but who will also bring it to completion at the day of Jesus Christ (Phil. 1:6). Community is a means by which God graciously transforms us into the image of his Son.

With all my heart, I plead with you not to be tempted with success, professionalism, or the fading fads of our entertainment-driven culture. Rather, pursue Jesus as the all-satisfying Treasure that he is, and feed his young sheep with the means God has provided. May the gospel of Christ fill your heart with grateful praise and guide your steps toward your heavenly home.

APPENDIX A

EVALUATING YOUR MINISTRY WITH YOUTH

WE HAVE NOTED that it is essential to acknowledge and teach that faithfulness to the Lord is always more important than "success" in ministry. As God's servants, we are to plant and water the gospel; God gives the growth (1 Cor. 3:7). But how would you evaluate your ministry to see whether planting and watering are truly happening? And is it wrong to want spiritual and numerical growth? The answers to those questions are the purpose of this appendix.

It should be clear by now that it is *God* who gives life, who regenerates the spiritually dead heart, and who quickens our affections to love and serve him (cf. Eph. 2:1–10). Why do so many youth programs seek numerical success and conversions as a sign of their ingenuity, programs, or "compelling" talks? I would like to say that we want numerical *success* "for God's glory" or "because we want more people to know Jesus." Indeed, I hope that is the case. However, for many, the ugly head of pride emerges more often than we would like. We want to be liked and accepted—by parents, peers, senior pastors, and even the youth themselves. Our pragmatic, results-obsessed culture has trained even youth workers to seek overall success as a *primary goal* rather than seeking "first the kingdom of God and his righteousness" (Matt. 6:33). Jesus teaches in Matthew 6 that when a believer seeks God's kingdom and righteousness, "all these things will be added to you." Many today, however, focus *first* on "all these things" rather than on God's kingdom and righteousness.

The apostle Paul teaches us that God's wisdom is different from worldly wisdom. What might be considered wise—even successful—in the world's eyes might be downright foolish in God's sight. He writes:

> For the word of the cross is folly to those who are perishing, but to us who are being saved it is the power of God. . . . For since, in the wisdom of God, the world did not know God through wisdom, it pleased God through the folly of what we preach to save those who believe. (1 Cor. 1:18, 21)

Notice that Paul calls it "the folly of what we preach." As God's new creation (2 Cor. 5:17) we labor in a kingdom not of this world, and so our values, judgments, and even evaluations of a youth ministry must be weighed in light of the revelation of God in his Word. There are three helpful ways to evaluate your youth ministry that maintain a healthy focus on God and his work through your planting and watering of the gospel, given here as three evaluative questions: Are you practicing the means of grace in your ministry? Do you and your ministry team have a greater knowledge and love for God? Do you see spiritual fruit in the lives of the youth?

ARE YOU PRACTICING THE MEANS OF GRACE?

The aim of this book has been to offer a plea for youth pastors, youth leaders, and parents to reclaim or (possibly) to discover a model of youth ministry focused on the Word of God, prayer, sacraments, service, and grace-centered community. One of the easiest ways to evaluate your ministry is to examine whether all of these are being communicated, taught, and practiced on a regular basis with the youth.

It might be helpful to sit down with some other youth leaders or parents and discuss where you see these five areas in your ministry or where you see the *potential* for them. For example, brainstorm ways to incorporate gospel-driven service projects into a regular pattern of ministry practice with your youth. It might also be helpful to take out a sheet of paper or your computer and organize a pattern or rotation of emphasizing different aspects of the sacraments or times of prayer.

It needs to be absolutely clear, however, that just because your ministry "teaches the Bible" doesn't necessarily mean that it teaches the *gospel*. Cults claim to "teach" the Bible. The gospel needs to be brought as much as possible into discipleship groups, lessons, and even playing sports with the youth. The gospel has several major parts:

1. God's holiness and character
2. Our sin and its "wages"—death
3. God's grace and love in sending his only Son to be our substitute on the cross to pay for our sin
4. We are saved by faith alone in the finished work of Christ alone, through whom we are counted "righteous" and "not guilty" before God because of forgiveness and his righteousness credited to us.

Good works should always be motivated by the gospel of Jesus Christ. In evaluating your ministry, you could ask whether your lessons and discussions do center on these gospel truths.

"Are we regularly engaged in prayer?" is another evaluative question. This is an evaluation of prayer in private (as youth leaders), prayer with other youth leaders, leading prayer in group settings, or having the youth pray for one another. Notice, however, that we are not evaluating the depth of the students' prayer life, although this needs to be taught and encouraged. We are to constantly remember that it is *God* who gives the growth of faith. But planting and watering the gospel in the lives of the youth are part of our task. One way to do this is by regularly making opportunities for prayer.

The same goes with teaching the importance of the sacraments, service, and grace-centered community. Do your youth have regular opportunity to learn and grow in these areas, and are they being *led* in these areas? While teaching is essential (and biblical!), we need to be leaders who also *inspire* our youth by how we live. If I always talk about how we need to minister to the poor and homeless but never do it myself, I am not planting and watering—either with great faithfulness to the Lord or with great effectiveness in ministry.

Once I was teaching through Hebrews 13 when I got to verse 3, "Remember those who are in prison, as though in prison with them." I had never been to a prison, nor had I talked with inmates. Notwithstanding the many prison ministries out there, I had never really thought about doing prison ministry. So, before I taught on that passage, I drove down and visited the local jail. I talked with the lieutenant on duty and asked questions about the inmates and what they eat, what they wear, and what kinds of activities they do. When I taught that night at youth group, I not only could relay the truth of the biblical teaching, but I could give some practical application for them from real-life experience that inspired them to go and do the same.

Wherever you find yourself in ministry, stop and evaluate your weekly, monthly, and yearly ministry to see whether the means of grace are regularly taught and practiced and that the ministry as a whole is gospel-focused.

DO YOU HAVE A GREATER KNOWLEDGE AND LOVE FOR GOD?

Knowledge transforms thinking; thinking transforms the heart; and the heart translates into action. The apostle Paul writes in Philippians:

> And it is my prayer that your love may abound more and more, with knowledge and all discernment, so that you may approve what is excellent, and so be pure and blameless for the day of Christ, filled with the fruit of righteousness that comes through Jesus Christ, to the glory and praise of God. (Phil. 1:9–11)

Notice the flow of these three verses. Paul is praying that the Philippians' love may abound more and more *with knowledge.* He echoes this in Romans 12:2, where he exhorts the Roman Christians: "be transformed by the renewal of your mind." Jesus relates knowledge to salvation when he prays, "And this is eternal life, that they know you the only true God, and Jesus Christ whom you have sent" (John 17:3). Knowledge is intimately related to a growing love for God.

One way to evaluate your ministry is to see whether *you* (and/or your ministry team) have a greater knowledge of and love for God. Do you love him for who he is: his character and attributes? Do you love his Word and long to be nourished by it? Do you want to seek him in prayer, to be led to the green pastures and still waters of his transformative grace?

One of the greatest ways to grow a love for God is by meditating on the character of God. For example, you could ask, "What does it mean that God is *holy* and why should that make a difference in how I live?" or "How does God being sovereign—in complete control over all things—inform or transform how I pray or how I respond to suffering? There are many ways to grow your love for God, but he has graciously given us these ways in what our study has centered on—*the means of grace.*

In evaluating your ministry, if you find that your own love for and knowledge of God have not grown, you might need to evaluate (1) your motives in ministry, (2) where your time is spent, and (3) your overall goal—whether being faithful to God is more important than being "successful" by worldly pressure.

DO YOU SEE SPIRITUAL FRUIT IN THE LIVES OF YOUR YOUTH?

You might wonder how this question could be a consistent evaluative question in light of the truth that it is *God* who gives the growth in a person's life. Our answer comes in the fact that Jesus teaches this as a right way to evaluate. He says that "the tree is known by its fruit" (Matt. 12:33). We are to "bear fruit" (Matt. 3:8), as healthy trees bear good fruit (Matt. 7:17). Paul gives us the "fruit of the Spirit" in Galatians 5:22–23: "But the fruit of the Spirit is love, joy, peace, patience, kindness, goodness, faithfulness, gentleness, self-control."

The amazing thing is that we are to evaluate professing believers (including youth) based on the spiritual fruit in their lives, recognizing that it is fruit *produced* by the Spirit. So how does this relate to evaluating "what you do" in your youth ministry? First, ask yourself and others involved whether they see spiritual growth/fruit in the lives of your youth. This might be an indicator of the priorities of ministry. While it is God who gives the growth, he has ordained growth to happen along with the ministry of the Word: "So faith comes from hearing, and hearing through the word of Christ" (Rom. 10:17). As God saves a person through the proclamation of the gospel—the means he has ordained for the elect to come to saving faith—so also he has ordained prayer as a means by which he acts in our lives.

If you are not seeing people saved in your ministry—thus, no spiritual fruit—then perhaps the gospel isn't being communicated. Evaluating spiritual fruit is therefore a good test of gospel-rich or gospel-poor ministry.

In a culture bent on seeing large numbers flood through your doors, and making *that* the priority of a ministry, let us strive to communicate, teach, and practice the means of grace and evaluate whether or not our ministries are set up to be guided by them. Evaluate whether you and your ministry team have a greater knowledge of and love for God. Finally, evaluate whether your youth exhibit spiritual fruit—remembering to give God the glory for growing them by his grace through the planting and watering of gospel ministry.

✍ APPENDIX B ✍

SHEPHERDING YOUTH ALONGSIDE FAMILIES AND CHURCH OFFICERS

MORE AND MORE youth ministries across America are becoming separate enclaves within the greater church body—detached huddles of teenage "mini-churches." These come complete with everything needed for a balanced spiritual diet—the three "Fs": food, fun, and fellowship. However, this approach is greatly mistaken and, to be honest, very dangerous.

As our culture has separated, defined, and categorized teens into their own separate world, it is absolutely necessary that we find ways to assimilate them into the greater church body so that the hands, feet, arms, and legs of Christ (metaphorically, of course) may appreciate and depend on one another. This thread has been explored in *Giving Up Gimmicks*, but here we need to consider how youth can be shepherded in a ministry that comes alongside the family and church leaders.

TACKLING SIN WITH PARENTS

The youth pastor or youth leader can often feel like he or she lives between the teenage and parent worlds. This becomes very apparent when the youth leader is dealing with a particular sin issue in a teen's life. I remember meeting with a youth whose parents had just become members at our church. We met at a Waffle House early in the morning before school and, over scrambled eggs, he told me that he was smoking weed. Then he said, "But don't tell my parents—they would *kill* me if they found out!"

So there I was faced with a decision. Do I keep his trust and not tell his parents or do I blow my ministry with him and spill the beans? My decision proved to be a poor one. I told him that *he* needed to tell his parents, and explained why they should know. He ended up agreeing with me and told me that he would do it. Where I failed is that I didn't follow up with him about it. He never told his parents, and one evening I received a call from his mother: "Brian, how could you have known that my son was using drugs and you not tell us, his parents?!" I learned my lesson.

But on the other hand, I've made the mistake of not going directly to the youth first. When I found out that a teen was beginning a physically charged relationship with his girlfriend, I went directly to the parents without talking with him. I lost his trust, and it took a couple of years to build it back.

You may or may not have a policy on dealing with a sin issue in a teen's life. Currently, when I hear of a sin issue, I go directly to the youth. If I feel that the parents need to know about it, I will give the youth one to two weeks (depending on the seriousness of the issue) to tell them. If not, then I tell them. I always offer to be there for the discussion or to help in any way that I can. I have been in many meetings where the youth and his or her parents were in the same room tackling a sin issue. It should be noted that, just because an adult parent is an adult parent, doesn't mean that he or she will always *act* like an adult parent. Sometimes parents need to be taught and trained in how to shepherd their teens.

SHEPHERDING YOUTH ALONGSIDE PARENTS

We have examined how youth leaders come alongside parents as they raise their children. To be sure, parents are the primary influencers in their children's lives, not youth pastors.[1] However, more and more youth are coming from broken homes, abusive backgrounds, and anti-Christian families. Other youth come from a long line of strong Christian believers and have (surprisingly) never known a non-Christian. While it is best to deal with each youth individually, there are some overarching ideas to help shepherd your youth as you partner with their parents.

First, get to know the parents. This might seem rather obvious, but building relationships with the parents takes time, communication, and thoughtfulness. For example, if the dad likes to go fishing, take him fishing. If the mom likes to go to Starbucks, go to Starbucks with her. However, be very careful not to do this with the opposite sex. Don't go to Starbucks, for example, with another man's wife! That might be the last cup of coffee you drink! But the point is to do things that can build those relationships, even if it means calling them up and talking over the phone. Ask them about their desires, fears, and hopes for their children, and what they are doing at home to see those things come to fruition.

Second, lead parents to the means of grace for their own spiritual growth.[2] Point them to the importance of reading and studying the Word, prayer, the sacraments, serving others, and being involved in the local church body. Point them to the necessity of Lord's Day worship and family worship. It cannot be stressed enough that a strong Christian home is the best ministry to youth. Do all you can to foster and encourage parents to avail themselves and their families of the riches of the gospel—communicated in and through God's means of grace.

Third, do things with both parents *and* their teenage children. For example, take them to serve at a local homeless shelter or go and play soccer on a Saturday morning. Pick something that you think they might all enjoy, especially the youth. If the son or daughter enjoys a certain activity (something the parent can do!), the parent will want to spend time building up that relationship. While spending this time together, look for ways to build up and encourage gospel growth in their lives. Ask them questions and lead them with brokenness—as you boast in the cross of Christ.

Fourth, have parents rotate through youth ministry positions (where possible) as leaders, activity chaperones, or simply coming to Sunday school. There is a wide variety of opinions on this point. Some insist on never separating youth and parents while others insist on never having them together. I try to maintain a balance. I don't exclude parents if they want to visit youth group or Sunday school. I always encourage them to be there, but I also encourage them to grow in a community of people their age as well. Wherever you find yourself in this polarity, it is important to remember connecting teens to parents and older adults. Building a multigenerational community not only fosters greater growth in all age groups, but also reflects the greater church body as a covenant community of believers.

Fifth, encourage your youth to change where they sit in worship. It would be good for them to sit with parents, but they might want to get to know other youth or other adults in the church. It needs to be pointed out, however, that they should probably be monitored to some degree so as not to be distracted or be a distraction for others. Too often, churches have separate "groups" based solely on where people sit on Sunday morning. While there are advantages to this, there are also disadvantages. Being intentional with meeting new people around you and building one another up in Christ on the Lord's Day is a great way to strengthen body life with parents, teens, and other adults.

SHEPHERDING YOUTH ALONGSIDE CHURCH OFFICERS

In his book *The Shepherd Leader*, Timothy Witmer has laid out an excellent biblical model for shepherding in the church.[3] Whether your church has elders, overseers, deacons, priests, bishops, or a group of lay leaders, it is important to work alongside these leaders in the shepherding of your youth.[4] Not only can this provide added spiritual care for the youth, but it backs up your ministry with them and can even disperse some of the shepherding load. Below are several ideas on how to shepherd youth in partnership with church leadership.

First, as Witmer contends, the overseers of the church should be striving to do some sort of shepherding of the sheep, on both a macro and a micro level. These levels include knowing the people, feeding the people through Word and sacrament, leading the people with vision and prayer, and protecting the people through instruction and discipline.[5] In our church, all members have shepherding elders who make contact with them on a regular basis. Those elders then report any issues requiring special pastoral care to the pastors, who follow up with both the elder and the member(s). In this way— at least ideally—all church members have shepherding elders they can go to in a time of need, who know them and have a desire to feed them through gospel ministry.

This basic structure can provide an enormous help in shepherding your youth. When an issue arises between a youth and his or her parents, for example, they can have the direct oversight and guidance of their shepherding elder. When a youth has surgery or there is a death in the family, I will often contact that youth's shepherding elder (the elder who is over their family) and have him get involved in the ministry to that family. In addition, there have been cases when I've been out of town or tied up and I really needed an elder to go to the hospital for a youth. It has been a wonderful blessing to call up that youth's shepherding elder and have him go for me.

Second, if you are a youth pastor or leader, you will undoubtedly get many phone calls and e-mails asking for you and the youth to "help out" in moving something, doing yard work, setting up chairs, etc. This can be a touchy issue between youth leaders and the other members. But if you can come alongside the deacons in coordinating some of these projects, you can utilize the deacons' vital ministry in the shepherding of your youth. Moreover, because the deacons have been charged with the physical ministry of the church, they have a better idea of what the body really needs and how youth can help with that need. They have the big picture and can usually determine how youth can best serve Christ toward that end.

While it is important to build up gospel-centered community among the youth in your local church, it is equally important to see the necessity and blessing of working alongside parents and church officers in their spiritual development. It is my hope that you will count this charge a joy and privilege as you strive for spiritual growth through God's means of grace.

NOTES

Chapter One: Why Entertainment Hasn't Worked

1. Doug Fields, *Purpose-Driven Youth Ministry* (Grand Rapids: Zondervan, 1998).

2. Ron Luce, *Battle Cry for a Generation: The Fight to Save America's Youth* (Colorado Springs: David C. Cook Publishing Co., 2005), 21. I have seen the numbers vary from 75 percent on the low end to Luce's estimation on the high end.

3. Alex and Brett Harris, *Do Hard Things: A Teenage Rebellion Against Low Expectations* (Colorado Springs: Multnomah, 2008).

4. This statistic is cited in many places, including Gary A. Goreham, "Denominational Comparison of Rural Youth Ministry Programs," *Review of Religious Research*, Vol. 45, No. 4 (June, 2004): 346–48, and youthworkermovement.org.

5. Kent and Barbara Hughes, *Liberating Ministry from the Success Syndrome* (Wheaton: Crossway Books, 2008).

Chapter Two: What Is a "Means of Grace" Ministry?

1. Robert L. Reymond, *A New Systematic Theology of the Christian Faith*, 2nd ed. (Nashville: Thomas Nelson Publishers, 1998), 913.

2. Literally, "by the work performed."

3. Though the number of "means" has traditionally been three, there has been disagreement within the Reformed community over the number. For example, Berkhof argues that there are only two: the preaching of the Word and the administration of the sacraments. See Louis Berkhof, *Systematic Theology* (Grand Rapids: William B. Eerdmans Publishing Company, 1996), 604. More recently, Harry Reeder lists six "means": Word, prayer, ministry, fellowship, evangelism, and

sacraments. See *The Leadership Dynamic: A Biblical Model for Raising Effective Leaders* (Wheaton: Crossway Books, 2008), 123–24.

4. For a thorough study of the means of grace in Reformed worship, see Hughes Oliphant Old, *Worship: Reformed According to Scripture*, revised and expanded edition (Louisville: Westminster John Knox Press, 2002).

5. Janie B. Cheaney, "Despising Our Youth," in *World* (September 25, 2010), 24.

6. See Brett McCracken, *Hipster Christianity: When Church and Cool Collide* (Grand Rapids: Baker Books, 2010), for a good critique of this all-too-common trend.

7. John D. Payne, *In the Splendor of Holiness: Rediscovering the Beauty of Reformed Worship for the 21st Century* (White Hall, WV: Tolle Lege Press, 2008), 15.

Chapter Three: Ministry of the Word

1. John Piper, *When the Darkness Will Not Lift: Doing What We Can While We Wait for God—and Joy* (Wheaton: Crossway Books, 2006), 61–62.

2. Daniel R. Hyde, *Welcome to a Reformed Church: A Guide for Pilgrims* (Orlando: Reformation Trust Publishing, 2010), 133.

3. John Calvin, *Institutes of the Christian Religion*, ed. John T. McNeill, trans. Ford Lewis Battles (Philadelphia: The Westminster Press, 1960), 1.7.4, 1.9.3.

4. Payne, *In the Splendor of Holiness*, 85.

5. Old, *Worship: Reformed According to Scripture*, 74.

6. That is, preaching through a book of the Bible, chapter by chapter, verse by verse—picking up where the minister left off the previous Lord's Day.

7. For a good study of the preaching ministry, see Bryan Chapell, *Christ-Centered Preaching: Redeeming the Expository Sermon* (Grand Rapids: Baker Academic, 2005), and D. Martyn Lloyd-Jones, *Preaching and Preachers* (Grand Rapids: Zondervan Publishing House, 1971).

8. Robert L. Dabney, *Discussions*, vol. 1, ed. C. R. Vaughan (Richmond, VA: Presbyterian Committee on Publication, 1890), 646. Interestingly enough, he called meditation a "means of grace."

9. John Bunyan, *The Pilgrim's Progress: From This World to That Which is to Come*, ed. C. J. Lovik (Wheaton: Crossway Books, 2009), 91–92.

10. Some of the principles in the first and fourth applications find their origin in John Piper, *Counted Righteous in Christ: Should We Abandon the Imputation of Christ's Righteousness?* (Wheaton: Crossway Books, 2002), 31.

11. O. C. Edwards Jr., *A History of Preaching* (Nashville: Abingdon Press, 2004), 286.

12. Charles Hodge, *Systematic Theology* (Peabody, MA: Hendrickson Publishers, 2008), 3:127–29.

13. Michael Horton, *The Gospel-Driven Life: Being Good News People in a Bad News World* (Grand Rapids: Baker Books, 2009), 193.

14. See John Piper, *Desiring God: Meditations of a Christian Hedonist* (Colorado Springs: Multnomah Books, 2003).

Chapter Four: Empowered through Prayer

1. Willem Teellinck, *The Path of True Godliness*, trans. Annemie Godbehere, ed. Joel R. Beeke (Grand Rapids: Reformation Heritage Books, 2003), 203.

2. A similar point was made by Job's three friends in response to his suffering.

3. "How Teenagers' Faith Practices are Changing" (poll found at http://www.barna.org/teens-next-gen-articles/403-how-teenagers-faith-practices-ares-changing).

4. Derek Prime and Alistair Begg, *On Being a Pastor: Understanding Our Calling and Work* (Chicago: Moody Publishers, 2004), 65.

5. Ibid.

6. John Charles Ryle, *Practical Religion* (Edinburgh: The Banner of Truth Trust, 1998), 63.

7. Prime and Begg, *On Being a Pastor*, 68.

8. D. G. Hart and John R. Muether, *With Reverence and Awe: Returning to the Basics of Reformed Worship* (Phillipsburg, NJ: P&R Publishing, 2002), 142.

9. I will discuss some practical and joy-filled ways to build a youth ministry team in chap. 8, "Building and Leading a Youth Ministry Team."

Chapter Five: Nourished in the Sacraments

1. The Nielson Company, "How Teens Use Media" (June 2009), 3.

2. Richard Pratt Jr., "Reformed View: Baptism as a Sacrament of the Covenant," in *Understanding Four Views on Baptism* (Grand Rapids: Zondervan, 2007), 59.

3. Sean Michael Lucas, *On Being Presbyterian* (Phillipsburg, NJ: P&R Publishing, 2006), 83.

4. Calvin, *Institutes of the Christian Religion*, 4.14.1.

5. Ibid.

6. Ibid., 4.14.3.

7. Keith A. Mathison, *Given For You: Reclaiming Calvin's Doctrine of the Lord's Supper* (Phillipsburg, NJ: P&R Publishing, 2002), 9.

8. Bryan Chapell, *Why Do We Baptize Infants?* (Phillipsburg, NJ: P&R Publishing, 2006), 11–12.

9. For a good overview of the blessing and warning in circumcision, see Mark E. Ross, "Baptism and Circumcision as Signs and Seals," in *The Case for Covenantal Infant Baptism*, ed. Gregg Strawbridge (Phillipsburg, NJ: P&R Publishing, 2003), 85–111.

10. The practice of sprinkling the blood on the people of Israel in the Old Testament, the sprinkling language present in the New Testament (cf. Heb. 13:9; 10:22), and the testimony of the early church all point to sprinkling as a biblical and primary mode of baptism for the church today. Many within the Reformed tradition, however, are open to immersion, seeing a biblical warrant in being buried with him in baptism and raised to walk in newness of life (Rom. 6:4).

11. Acts 10:47–48; 16:15, 30–31; 18:8; 1 Cor. 1:14, 16.

12. Chapell, *Why Do We Baptize Infants?* 15.

13. The Barna Group, "Report Examines the State of Mainline Protestant Churches" (December, 2009).

14. The free offer of the gospel is seen by some as running contrary to the doctrine of election. However, it is the means by which God brings the elect to saving faith. Luke writes in Acts 13:48, "And when the Gentiles heard [the gospel], they began rejoicing and glorifying the word of the Lord, and as many as were appointed to eternal life believed."

15. As seen in many Lutheran churches.

16. Mathison, *Given for You*, 260.

17. The phrase, "fencing the table," is used to describe the biblical warnings given about how we approach the Lord's Supper. These include warnings for the unbeliever and the unrepentant.

Chapter Six: Satisfied by Service

1. A helpful study is John Piper, *Brothers, We Are Not Professionals: A Plea to Pastors for Radical Ministry* (Nashville: B&H, 2002).

2. Christian Smith and Melinda Lundquist Denton, *Soul Searching: The Religious and Spiritual Lives of American Teenagers* (New York; Oxford: Oxford University Press, 2009), 163.

3. Ibid., 163–71.

4. C. S. Lewis, *Weight of Glory* (New York: Harper Collins Publishers, 2001), 26.

5. Harry L. Reeder III with Rod Gragg, *The Leadership Dynamic: A Biblical Model for Raising Effective Leaders* (Wheaton: Crossway Books, 2008), 120–21.

6. The King James Version even translates the Greek word, *latreia*, "service."

7. Steve Corbett and Brian Fikkert, *When Helping Hurts: How to Alleviate Poverty Without Hurting the Poor and Yourself* (Chicago: Moody Publishers, 2009), 175.

8. Ibid., 177.

9. One of the best I've seen is Timothy J. Keller, *Ministries of Mercy: The Call of the Jericho Road*, 2nd Ed. (Phillipsburg, NJ: P&R Publishing, 1997).

Chapter Seven: Transformed through Community

1. Horton, *The Gospel-Driven Life*, 194–95.

2. Bryan Chapell, *Holiness by Grace: Delighting in the Joy that Is Our Strength* (Wheaton: Crossway Books, 2001), 8.

3. Cf. Westminster Shorter Catechism, Q. 35.

4. Philip Graham Ryken, *The Communion of Saints: Living in Fellowship with the People of God* (Phillipsburg, NJ: P&R Publishing, 2001), 9–10.

5. Timothy Keller, *Gospel in Life: Grace Changes Everything* (Grand Rapids: Zondervan, 2010), 59–70.

6. The Greek word, *proslambanomai*, means "to accept" or "to receive."

7. Dan B. Allender, *The Healing Path: How the Hurts in Your Past Can Lead You to a More Abundant Life* (Colorado Springs: WaterBrook Press, 1999), 248.

8. Keller, *Gospel in Life*, 59.

9. Allender, *The Healing Path*, 250.

10. Joel R. Beeke, *Puritan Reformed Spirituality: A Practical Theological Study from Our Reformed and Puritan Heritage* (Darlington, England: Evangelical Press, 2006), 8.

11. Ibid., 410.

12. This is what has traditionally been referred to as Calvin's third use of the law.

13. John Owen, *The Mortification of Sin* (Ross-Shire, Scotland: Christian Focus, 1996), 20.

14. J. C. Ryle, *Practical Religion*, 441.

Chapter Eight: Building and Leading a Youth Ministry Team

1. If there were serious schisms caused by the previous youth pastor, caution is needed. But, if possible, don't create schism and disunity in the attempt to look better than the previous minister.

2. Fields, *Purpose-Driven Youth Ministry*, 17.

Appendix B: Shepherding Youth Alongside Families and Church Officers

1. Unless the child is adopted or doesn't know his or her parents for one reason or another.

2. For a good study on gospel parenting, see William P. Farley, *Gospel-Powered Parenting: How the Gospel Shapes and Transforms Parenting* (Phillipsburg, NJ: P&R Publishing, 2009).

3. Timothy Z. Witmer, *The Shepherd Leader: Achieving Effective Shepherding in Your Church* (Phillipsburg, NJ: P&R Publishing, 2010). Some of the ideas in this chapter build off the overall trajectory and vision of shepherding as outlined in *The Shepherd Leader*.

4. Ideally, your church will have men who hold the two biblical offices of elder and deacon. For some studies on these offices, see Michael Brown, ed., *Called to Serve: Essays for Elders and Deacons* (Wyoming, MI: Reformed Fellowship, 2007); Cornelius Van Dam, *The Elder: Today's Ministry Rooted in All of Scripture* (Phillipsburg, NJ: P&R Publishing, 2009); and Henry Webb, *Deacons: Servant Models in the Church* (Nashville: B&H Books, 2001).

5. Witmer, *The Shepherd Leader*, 189.

INDEX OF SUBJECTS
AND NAMES

Brian H. Cosby (BA, Samford University; MDiv, Beeson Divinity School; DMin, The North American Reformed Seminary) is an ordained minister in the Presbyterian Church in America and serves as associate pastor of youth and families at Carriage Lane Presbyterian Church in Peachtree City, Georgia. He is the author of several books and continues to write for various journals and magazines. He and his family make their home in Fayetteville, Georgia.

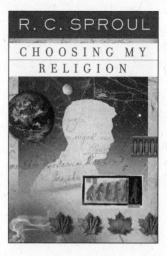

Christians are often unaware when they adopt non-Christian ideas. This book examines seven non-Christian ideas that cripple the Christian mind.

"Like a good doctor, Selvaggio does not rail at us about our illness; he aims to heal and so offers solutions in Christ. Whether you are a teenager, a mother, a businessman, or a pastor, this book will bring health to your soul and equip you to live soberly, righteously, and godly in this present world."
—**Joel R. Beeke**

Religion shapes your loves, ideals, behavior, and goals, but unless you've thought about it clearly, your religion may not be worth believing. *Choosing My Religion* will help readers in their late teens and early twenties arrive at sound answers to life's big questions.

"A profound book, bringing great truths of Scripture into the real world."
—**Steve Camp**

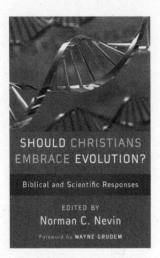

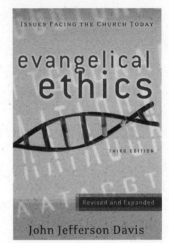

Thirteen scientists and theologians set out a clear framework for relevant biblical, theological, and scientific issues and answer crucial questions.

"The experts in science and theology who have contributed chapters to *Should Christians Embrace Evolution?* are of the trustworthy kind, and their words of wisdom will be very helpful to Christians who are struggling to sort out conflicting claims and arrive at the truth."
—**Phillip E. Johnson**

John Jefferson Davis brings mature biblical thought to issues such as homosexuality, genetics, abortion, euthanasia, war and peace, the environment, divorce, and remarriage.

"The subject is timely, the research careful, the presentation passionate, and the viewpoints with which the author differs are honestly represented. . . . The reference sources alone are worth the price of the book."
—*Bookstore Journal*

"Why do I keep on sinning?" This book takes dead aim at the heart of ongoing sin. Drawing from two masterful works by John Owen, Kris Lundgaard offers insight, encouragement, and hope for overcoming the enemy within.

"A delightful book. It is honest, real, and, best of all, hopeful."
—Steve Brown

Many teens are active in church youth programs, but drop out of church later in life and never return. Other young adults merely rest on the merits of their parents' faith. Graustein and Jacobsen remind teenagers in Christian homes of their blessings, suggest practical ways to avoid common dangers, and urge them to think and live in a manner that pleases God.

"[This] book is one that can shake teenagers and parents out of a false sense of safety and ignite a much-needed spiritual passion."
—Joshua Harris

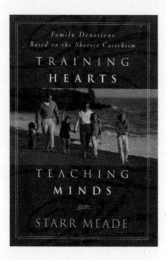

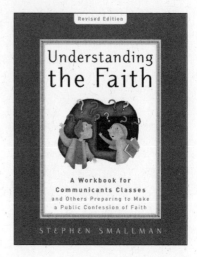

This book of daily readings explains the Shorter Catechism in simple language. Six brief meditations address the main points of each question, allowing time for discussion and review. Useful for church, classroom, or home.

"Provides the practical resources to infuse family devotions with meaning, purpose, and lively joy. This is a book that every family will want to have and use."
—**George Grant**

This workbook walks students through the essentials of the Christian faith, modeling the format of the Westminster Shorter Catechism in modern English.

"It is important that my children know the scriptural reasons for what we believe. It is not enough for them to recite facts; they need to know why we believe what we do. *Understanding the Faith* is an excellent tool for accomplishing this purpose."
—**Cynthia Delvecchio**